Junior Great Books

SERIES 5

BOOK TWO

◆   ◆   ◆

The Interpretive discussion program that moves

students toward excellence in reading comprehension,

critical thinking, and writing

JUNIOR GREAT BOOKS®

SERIES 5   BOOK TWO

THE GREAT BOOKS FOUNDATION
A nonprofit educational organization

Junior Great Books® is a registered trademark of the Great Books Foundation. Shared Inquiry™ is a trademark of the Great Books Foundation. The contents of this publication include proprietary trademarks and copyrighted materials, and may be used or quoted only with permission and appropriate credit to the Foundation.

9   8   7   6   5   4   3   2

Printed in the United States of America

Published and distributed by

THE GREAT BOOKS FOUNDATION
A nonprofit educational organization

35 East Wacker Drive, Suite 400

Chicago, IL 60601

CONTENTS

CHARLES

Shirley Jackson

The day my son Laurie started kindergarten he renounced corduroy overalls with bibs and began wearing blue jeans with a belt; I watched him go off the first morning with the older girl next door, seeing clearly that an era of my life was ended, my sweet-voiced nursery-school tot replaced by a long-trousered, swaggering character who forgot to stop at the corner and wave goodbye to me.

He came home the same way, the front door slamming open, his cap on the floor, and the voice suddenly become raucous shouting, "Isn't anybody *here*?"

At lunch he spoke insolently to his father, spilled his baby sister's milk, and remarked that his teacher said we were not to take the name of the Lord in vain.

"How *was* school today?" I asked, elaborately casual.

"All right," he said.

"Did you learn anything?" his father asked.

Laurie regarded his father coldly. "I didn't learn nothing," he said.

"Anything," I said. "Didn't learn anything."

"The teacher spanked a boy, though," Laurie said, addressing his bread and butter. "For being fresh," he added, with his mouth full.

"What did he do?" I asked. "Who was it?"

Laurie thought. "It was Charles," he said. "He was fresh. The teacher spanked him and made him stand in a corner. He was awfully fresh."

"What did he do?" I asked again, but Laurie slid off his chair, took a cookie, and left, while his father was still saying, "See here, young man."

The next day Laurie remarked at lunch, as soon as he sat down, "Well, Charles was bad again today." He grinned enormously and said, "Today Charles hit the teacher."

"Good heavens," I said, mindful of the Lord's name, "I suppose he got spanked again?"

"He sure did," Laurie said. "Look up," he said to his father.

"What?" his father said, looking up.

"Look down," Laurie said. "Look at my thumb. Gee, you're dumb." He began to laugh insanely.

"Why did Charles hit the teacher?" I asked quickly.

"Because she tried to make him color with red crayons," Laurie said. "Charles wanted to color with green crayons so he hit the teacher and she spanked him and said nobody play with Charles but everybody did."

The third day—it was Wednesday of the first week—Charles bounced a see-saw onto the head of a little girl and made her bleed, and the teacher made him stay inside all during recess. Thursday Charles had to stand in a corner during story time because he kept pounding his feet on the floor. Friday Charles was deprived of blackboard privileges because he threw chalk.

On Saturday I remarked to my husband, "Do you think kindergarten is too unsettling for Laurie? All this toughness, and bad grammar, and this Charles boy sounds like such a bad influence."

"It'll be all right," my husband said reassuringly. "Bound to be people like Charles in the world. Might as well meet them now as later."

On Monday Laurie came home late, full of news. "Charles," he shouted as he came up the hill; I was waiting anxiously on the front steps. "Charles," Laurie yelled all the way up the hill, "Charles was bad again."

"Come right in," I said, as soon as he came close enough. "Lunch is waiting."

"You know what Charles did?" he demanded, following me through the door. "Charles yelled so in school they sent a boy in from first grade to tell the teacher she had to make Charles keep quiet, and so

9

Charles had to stay after school. And so all the children stayed to watch him."

"What did he do?" I asked.

"He just sat there," Laurie said, climbing into his chair at the table. "Hi, Pop, y'old dust mop."

"Charles had to stay after school today," I told my husband. "Everyone stayed with him."

"What does this Charles look like?" my husband asked Laurie. "What's his other name?"

"He's bigger than me," Laurie said. "And he doesn't have any rubbers and he doesn't ever wear a jacket."

Monday night was the first Parent-Teachers meeting, and only the fact that the baby had a cold kept me from going; I wanted passionately to meet Charles's mother. On Tuesday Laurie remarked suddenly, "Our teacher had a friend come to see her in school today."

"Charles's mother?" my husband and I asked simultaneously.

"Naaah," Laurie said scornfully. "It was a man who came and made us do exercises; we had to touch our toes. Look." He climbed down from his chair and squatted down and touched his toes. "Like this," he said. He got solemnly back into his chair and said, picking up his fork, "Charles didn't even *do* exercises."

"That's fine," I said heartily. "Didn't Charles want to do exercises?"

"Naaah," Laurie said. "Charles was so fresh to the teacher's friend he wasn't *let* do exercises."

"Fresh again?" I said.

"He kicked the teacher's friend," Laurie said. "The teacher's friend told Charles to touch his toes like I just did and Charles kicked him."

"What are they going to do about Charles, do you suppose?" Laurie's father asked him.

Laurie shrugged elaborately. "Throw him out of school, I guess," he said.

Wednesday and Thursday were routine; Charles yelled during story hour and hit a boy in the stomach and made him cry. On Friday Charles stayed after school again and so did all the other children.

With the third week of kindergarten Charles was an institution in our family; the baby was being a Charles when she cried all afternoon; Laurie did a Charles when he filled his wagon full of mud and pulled it through the kitchen; even my husband, when he caught his elbow in the telephone cord and pulled telephone, ashtray, and a bowl of flowers off the table, said, after the first minute, "Looks like Charles."

During the third and fourth weeks it looked like a reformation in Charles; Laurie reported grimly at lunch on Thursday of the third week, "Charles was so good today the teacher gave him an apple."

"What?" I said, and my husband added warily, "You mean Charles?"

"Charles," Laurie said. "He gave the crayons around and he picked up the books afterward and the teacher said he was her helper."

"What happened?" I asked incredulously.

"He was her helper, that's all," Laurie said, and shrugged.

"Can this be true, about Charles?" I asked my husband that night. "Can something like this happen?"

"Wait and see," my husband said cynically. "When you've got a Charles to deal with, this may mean he's only plotting."

He seemed to be wrong. For over a week Charles was the teacher's helper; each day he handed things out and he picked things up; no one had to stay after school.

"The P.T.A. meeting's next week again," I told my husband one evening. "I'm going to find Charles's mother there."

"Ask her what happened to Charles," my husband said. "I'd like to know."

"I'd like to know myself," I said.

On Friday of that week things were back to normal. "You know what Charles did today?" Laurie demanded at the lunch table, in a voice slightly awed. "He told a little girl to say a word and she said it and the teacher washed her mouth out with soap and Charles laughed."

"What word?" his father asked unwisely, and Laurie said, "I'll have to whisper it to you, it's so bad." He got down off his chair and went around to his father. His father bent his head down and Laurie whispered joyfully. His father's eyes widened.

"Did Charles tell the little girl to say *that*?" he asked respectfully.

"She said it *twice*," Laurie said. "Charles told her to say it *twice*."

"What happened to Charles?" my husband asked.

"Nothing," Laurie said. "He was passing out the crayons."

Monday morning Charles abandoned the little girl and said the evil word himself three or four times, getting his mouth washed out with soap each time. He also threw chalk.

My husband came to the door with me that evening as I set out for the P.T.A. meeting. "Invite her over for a cup of tea after the meeting," he said. "I want to get a look at her."

"If only she's there," I said prayerfully.

"She'll be there," my husband said. "I don't see how they could hold a P.T.A. meeting without Charles's mother."

At the meeting I sat restlessly, scanning each comfortable matronly face, trying to determine which one hid the secret of Charles. None of them looked to me haggard enough. No one stood up in the meeting and apologized for the way her son had been acting. No one mentioned Charles.

After the meeting I identified and sought out Laurie's kindergarten teacher. She had a plate with a cup of tea and a piece of chocolate cake; I had a plate with a cup of tea and a piece of marshmallow cake. We maneuvered up to one another cautiously and smiled.

"I've been so anxious to meet you," I said. "I'm Laurie's mother."

"We're all so interested in Laurie," she said.

"Well, he certainly likes kindergarten," I said. "He talks about it all the time."

"We had a little trouble adjusting, the first week or so," she said primly, "but now he's a fine little helper. With occasional lapses, of course."

"Laurie usually adjusts very quickly," I said. "I suppose this time it's Charles's influence."

"Charles?"

"Yes," I said, laughing, "you must have your hands full in that kindergarten, with Charles."

"Charles?" she said. "We don't have any Charles in the kindergarten."

A Bad Road for Cats

Cynthia Rylant

Louie! Louis! Where are you?"

The woman called it out again and again as she walked along Route 6. A bad road for cats. She prayed he hadn't wandered this far. But it had been nearly two weeks, and still Louis hadn't come home.

She stopped at a Shell station, striding up to the young man at the register. Her eyes snapped black and fiery as she spit the question at him:

"Have you seen a *cat*?" The word *cat* came out hard as a rock.

The young man straightened up.

"No, ma'am. No cats around here. Somebody dropped a mutt off a couple nights ago, but a Mack truck got it yesterday about noon. Dog didn't have a chance."

The woman's eyes pinched his.

"I lost my cat. Orange and white. If you see him, you be more careful of him than that dog. This is a bad road for cats."

15

She marched toward the door.

"I'll be back," she said, like a threat, and the young man straightened up again as she went out.

"Louie! Louis! Where are you?"

She was a very tall woman, and skinny. Her black hair was long and shiny, like an Indian's. She might have been a Cherokee making her way alongside a river, alert and watchful. Tracking.

But Route 6 was no river. It was a truckers' road, lined with gas stations, motels, dairy bars, diners. A nasty road, smelling of diesel and rubber.

The woman's name was Magda. And she was of French blood, not Indian. Magda was not old, but she carried herself as a very old and strong person might, with no fear of death and with a clear sense of her right to the earth and a disdain for the ugliness of belching machines and concrete.

Magda lived in a small house about two miles off Route 6. There she worked at a loom, weaving wool gathered from the sheep she owned. Magda's husband was dead, and she had no children. Only a cat named Louis.

Dunh. Dunh. Duuunnh.

Magda's heart pounded as a tank truck roared by. *Duuunnh.* The horn hurt her ears, making her feel sick inside, stealing some of her strength.

Four years before, Magda had found Louis at one of the gas stations on Route 6. She had been on her way home from her weekly trip to the grocery and had pulled in for a fill-up. As she'd stood inside the station in front of the cigarette machine, dropping in quarters, she'd felt warm fur against her leg and had given a start. Looking down, she'd seen an orange and white kitten. It had purred and meowed and pushed its nose into Magda's shoes. Smiling, Magda had picked the kitten up. Then she had seen the horror.

Half of the kitten's tail was gone. What remained was bloody and scabbed, and the stump stuck straight out.

Magda had carried the animal to one of the station attendants.

"Whose kitten is this?" Her eyes drilled in the question.

The attendant had shrugged his shoulders.

"Nobody's. Just a drop-off."

Magda had moved closer to him.

"What happened to its *tail*?" she asked, the words slow and clear.

"Got caught in the door. Stupid cat was under everybody's feet—no wonder half its tail got whacked."

Magda could not believe such a thing.

"And you offer it no *help*?" she had asked.

"Not my cat," he answered.

Magda's face had blazed as she'd turned and stalked out the door with the kitten.

A veterinarian mended what was left of the kitten's tail. And Magda named it Louis for her grandfather.

"Louie! Louis! Where are you?"

Dunh. Duuunnh. Another horn at her back. Magda wondered about her decision to walk Route 6 rather than drive it. She had thought that on foot she might find

Louis more easily—in a ditch, under some bushes, up a tree. They were even, she and Louis, if she were on foot, too. But the trucks were making her misery worse.

Magda saw a dairy bar up ahead. She thought she would stop and rest. She would have some coffee and a slice of quiet away from the road.

She walked across the wide gravel lot to the tiny walk-up window. Pictures of strawberry sundaes, spongy shakes, cones with curly peaks were plastered all over the building, drawing business from the road with big red words like *CHILLY*.

Magda barely glanced at the young girl working inside. All teenage girls looked alike to her.

"Coffee," she ordered.

"Black?"

"Yes."

Magda moved to one side and leaned against the building. The trucks were rolling out on the highway, but far enough away to give her time to regain her strength. No horns, no smoke, no dirt. A little peace.

She drank her coffee and thought about Louis when he was a kitten. Once, he had leaped from her attic window and she had found him, stunned and shivering, on the hard gravel below. The veterinarian said Louis had broken a leg and was lucky to be alive. The kitten had stomped around in a cast for a few weeks. Magda drew funny faces on it to cheer him up.

Louis loved white cheese, tall grass, and the skeins of wool Magda left lying around her loom.

That's what she would miss most, she thought, if Louis never came back: an orange and white cat making the yarn fly under her loom.

Magda finished her coffee, then turned to throw the empty cup in the trash can. As she did, a little sign in the bottom corner of the window caught her eye. The words were surrounded by dirty smudges:

4 Sal. CAT

Magda caught her breath. She moved up to the window and this time looked squarely into the face of the girl.

"Are you selling a *cat*?" she said quietly, but hard on *cat*.

"Not me. This boy," the girl answered, brushing her stringy hair back from her face.

"Where is he?" Magda asked.

"That yellow house right off the road up there."

Magda headed across the lot.

She had to knock only once. The door opened and standing there was a boy about fifteen.

"I saw your sign," Magda said. "I am interested in your cat."

The boy did not answer. He looked at Magda's face with his wide blue eyes, and he grinned, showing a mouth of rotten and missing teeth.

Magda felt a chill move over her.

"The cat," she repeated. "You have one to sell? Is it orange and white?"

The boy stopped grinning. Without a word, he slammed the door in Magda's face.

She was stunned. A strong woman like her, to be so stunned by a boy. It shamed her. But again she knocked on the door—and very hard this time.

No answer.

What kind of boy is this? Magda asked herself. A strange one. And she feared he had Louis.

She had just raised her hand to knock a third time when the door opened. There the boy stood with Louis in his arms.

Again, Magda was stunned. Her cat was covered with oil and dirt. He was thin, and his head hung weakly. When he saw Magda, he seemed to use his last bit of strength to let go a pleading cry.

The boy no longer was grinning. He held Louis close against him, forcefully stroking the cat's ears again and again and again. The boy's eyes were full of tears, his mouth twisted into sad protest.

Magda wanted to leap for Louis, steal him, and run for home. But she knew better. This was an unusual boy. She must be careful.

Magda put her hand into her pocket and pulled out a dollar bill.

"*Enough?*" she asked, holding it up.

The boy clutched the cat harder, his mouth puckering fiercely.

Magda pulled out two more dollar bills. She held the money up, the question in her eyes.

The boy relaxed his hold on Louis. He tilted his head to one side, as if considering Magda's offer.

Then, in desperation, Magda pulled out a twenty-dollar bill.

"*Enough?*" she almost screamed.

The boy's head jerked upright, then he grabbed all the bills with one hand and shoved Louis at Magda with the other.

Magda cradled Louis in her arms, rubbing her cheek across his head. Before walking away, she looked once more at the boy. He stood stiffly with the money clenched in his hand, tears running from his eyes and dripping off his face like rainwater.

Magda took Louis home. She washed him and healed him. And for many days she was in a rage at the strange boy who had sold her her own cat, nearly dead.

When Louis was healthy, though, and his old fat self, playing games among the yarn beneath her loom, her rage grew smaller and smaller until finally she could forgive the strange boy.

She came to feel sympathy for him, remembering his tears. And she wove some orange and white wool into a pattern, stuffed it with cotton, sewed two green button eyes and a small pink mouth onto it, then attached a matching stub of a tail.

She put the gift in a paper bag, and, on her way to the grocery one day, she dropped the bag in front of the boy's yellow house.

PODHU AND ARUWA

African folktale
as told by Humphrey Harman

Old Ramogi lived with all his family by the shores of the Great Lake. And what a family! There was Ramogi's wife, and his seven sons: Onyango and Ouma and Agwanda and Obwavo and Oyako and Podhu and Aruwa. Then *all* the sons were married and so there were seven wives and a swarm of small brown naked children *and* half a dozen poor relations and . . . and . . . and . . . More like a village than a family. Dozens of solid little houses with mud walls and yellow thatch and round them all a big hedge of *ojuok* and, outside that, gardens full of maize and millet and beans, and herds of cattle grazing in the water meadows, and bands of young men hunting deer and pig in the reeds.

Of course, with so many people living on top of one another, one could expect arguments and rows and so indeed there were, little ones all the time but sometimes big ones when everybody shouted for hours. Then, when a pot had been broken and someone had lost his temper properly and reached for a spear, Ramogi would bellow from the house where he was resting and that would be that, and everyone would be quiet until the next time. He was the head of the family and you did as you were told or you could go and carve yourself a field out of the Great Forest and live by yourself.

No one wanted to do that.

The Great Forest began a mile away to the east, very dark, very secret, full of strange sounds at night. It was a threatening place and mixed up with magic of the worst kind. The Elephant Folk lived there and the family of Ramogi left it strictly alone, for no one wishes to be turned into a tree or an ape or wander forever lost in a place where the sunlight is strained through so many leaves that it hardly reaches the ground.

On the other side of the village was a hill that was covered with rocks. But this was a cheerful place and was called Ramogi; and whether the hill was named after the man or the man after the hill no one was quite sure, and indeed, the matter was one for much argument on hot afternoons in the shade of a tree when the crops were in and nobody had much to do. Ramogi could have cleared the matter up perhaps, but he preferred to leave it alone, believing that it kept everyone harmlessly occupied and out of mischief.

Well, Ramogi had lived a good life but in the end he grew old and died, and Onyango, the eldest son, took his place and then it was time for all the other brothers to move on and make villages of their own. For although one usually listens to a father when he tells you to behave, no one takes much notice of a brother. And so they moved, going west along the lake or north into the plain, but not east, for that was toward the Great Forest. You couldn't go south unless you had webbed feet and anyone who has listened properly can understand why.

All the brothers went singly with their wives and children and followers and all of them settled on good land and built strong houses and did well, and since five of them don't come into this story again, we needn't bother about them anymore.

Except for Podhu and Aruwa, the youngest. They loved each other so dearly that each was unhappy if he did not know where the other was. Always they had been together. As little boys they had watched Ramogi's cows in the pasture and made their own toy cows out of wet clay from the ant heaps. At night they curled asleep on the same skin, and when they were bigger they hunted together. They had married sisters. Always they did the same things and thought the same thoughts, and sometimes one would start a sentence and stop and the other would finish it without hesitation. Generally people considered them as one person, which was sometimes awkward for their wives, because if you borrowed something from one brother's house and returned it to the other it could lead to misunderstanding.

And so when all their brothers had gone, except Onyango, who was asking pointed questions about when they expected to move, Podhu looked at Aruwa and Aruwa looked at Podhu and then Podhu said:

"Brother, it is time we also were going to look for land of our own."

Aruwa was busy covering the two mouths of a small drum with well-scraped skin and had got to the ticklish bit where you lace the skin tightly, and although you hold the drum with your feet and one hand and pull one thong with the other and another with your teeth, you could really do with two more hands. So he took a long time answering and it came out in jerks.

"Mm . . . yes . . . (mumble, mumble) . . . hold this thong a moment, Brother . . . yes, indeed . . . which direction . . . bother the thing! . . . ah, that's better . . . which direction did *you* think of going, Brother?"

"Well," said Podhu, "it's a mite difficult."

He began ticking off names on his fingers.

"Agwanda and Ouma have gone along the lake shore and so *they* won't want anyone else there. And Obwavo and Oyako have gone north and anyway, I never did think much of that plains country. I thought of going east."

"Into the forest, Brother?"

"*Beside* the forest, Aruwa. There's good land there running right down to the lake and plenty of wood at hand for the houses."

Aruwa finished knotting the thongs, put the drum between his knees, and tapped a little tune. He was a good musician.

25

"You know, Podhu," he said, shutting his eyes to listen to his own music, "I had something of the same idea. But is there room for two?"

Podhu considered.

"Not for two farms. Hardly enough for that. There would be enough for one big farm if we lived together."

Aruwa opened his eyes and looked at the sky and said to no one in particular:

"There is a saying among our people that although even cats and dogs can live peaceably together, brothers never can."

"I know," said Podhu, "but I thought we might try."

"An excellent idea," replied Aruwa. "We'll go east, to the Great Forest."

And so, very shortly afterward, they did, and built their house just where the forest became thin and gave up and turned to grass, and everything went so well with them that "to agree like Podhu and Aruwa" began to be a saying in that part of the world.

All might have gone on well if it hadn't been for Aruwa's magic spear.

Before Ramogi died he gave one thing of his possessions to each of his sons. Onyango got his feathered headdress, Ouma his flywhisk made from a cow's tail. Aruwa had been given a spear.

Ramogi had had many spears and this was not the one he used for hunting before he grew too stiff in the legs, or any of the half a dozen that lay across the rafters of his house and were borrowed by the boys when they became old enough to use them. This was an old, old spear that had belonged to Ramogi's father and his father before that and had been made by the smiths of a people called the Nandi who were skilled in all kinds of ironwork. It had a long narrow blade shaped like a reed, and Ramogi had treasured it and never permitted any of his sons to touch it. When they had asked why, he had always told them it was a magic spear and they had believed him. It became Aruwa's most treasured possession and leaned against the center post in the new house that he shared with Podhu.

One morning, when they had lived in their new house for a year and the season was at its height and the maize stood straight and stiff in the fields like soldiers, the tassels wet with dew, Aruwa drove the cattle out and Podhu stayed home and slept late.

He was awakened by cries from the women and behind all this noise a splashy sound of green maize stalks being crushed.

He sat for a moment, muddled with sleep, and then he made out words from the cries.

"Elephants! The Elephant Folk are in the maize!"

Podhu jumped up and seized a spear (it was Aruwa's precious one), ran out of the house, through the gateway in a moment, leapt a thorn hedge into the maize, and then stopped suddenly. The field seemed full of elephants. With their great backs shiny black with dew and wide ears spread, they forged through the maize like ships and the wet stalks smashed beneath them. Dozens of elephants, each spoiling more than a man could eat in a year, tearing

27

it up by sheaves with their wicked, snaky trunks and stuffing it into their mouths.

Podhu lost his temper and became reckless. He ran through the maize until he reached the edge of the desert of smashed plants, burst into the open, and gave a great yell of rage. There was a sudden silence. Every elephant stood stock-still and their great heads turned and regarded Podhu with grave amazement.

Then he flung Aruwa's spear with all his strength at the biggest elephant. He saw it stick in a wrinkled side and at that all the herd turned, screaming with anger and panic, stamped flat a hedge in their way, and crashed off into the forest . . . and on, on . . . the noise fading . . . until at last it vanished.

And with it Aruwa's spear.

As a matter of fact, when the elephants were out of sight of Podhu they stopped, pulled themselves together, and were more than a little ashamed. They took the spear out of the old bull, who grumbled dreadfully but was not much hurt, and then they took it back to the great clearing, deep in the forest, which was their home and which no one had ever found. There they stored the spear carefully with the other things they had picked up in their wanderings. Elephants are wasteful only about people's crops; they can be very economical about other things.

When Aruwa came home with the cattle, tired and hungry, his wife told him about the spear. He was furious. His precious spear gone off, stuck in the hide of an elephant! Were there not a dozen other spears of no particular value to throw at elephants if that was what Podhu wanted to do?

Podhu said that he was sorry.

Aruwa muttered under his breath and went to the edge of the forest to see if the spear had been knocked out against a tree. There was no spear, and the sight of the ruined maize didn't improve his temper.

Podhu, who was very hurt, offered to buy him the best spear that could be made in the country.

Aruwa shouted, "I want my father's magic spear and only that. I'll not forget it if you give me the whole world. And if you don't bring it back, I will kill you!"

"Very well," said Podhu, "I will get it or die in the attempt."

"You'll get it," sneered Aruwa. "And how? I suppose you will go and ask the elephants for it back?"

"Yes," said Podhu. "I will do exactly that."

That night everyone went to bed in the kind of sulky silence that follows a big family row.

The very next morning, before anyone else was awake, Podhu took a spear, slung a skin bag over one shoulder, and leaving the house, walked to the forest. At its edge he took one last look at the morning sun rising over the lake shore and then he grasped his spear firmly and pushed his way in among the trees.

There all was cold and green and gloomy, like a fish's world at the bottom of a pond. He found paths made by wild pigs and timid deer, and these he followed, his feet silent on the wet leaves. All that day he walked, going deeper and deeper until he knew he was where no man had been before, but still he found no sign of the Elephant Folk.

At last it grew even darker, and although he could not see it, he knew that the sun was setting. He found a tree whose great roots writhed from halfway up its trunk and fell in gigantic careless coils on the forest floor and, crawling in amongst these, he discovered a hollow full of dry leaves. In this he sat and ate his cold maize cake and then tried to sleep. Light vanished and the forest, so silent all day, grew full of noises: rustlings and croaking sounds, the hooting of owls, once a mysterious scream from high above his head and another time the heavy trampling of something big. Podhu trembled with cold and fear and at any moment expected to find himself changed into something unpleasant.

At last he slept and when he awoke it was as light as it ever got in that forest, and he stretched and finished his food and went on his way. Many hours later he came to a track which, it seemed to him, had not been made by an animal. He followed it slowly to a small clearing in the trees, and there he found a tumble-down hut with the smoke of a cooking fire streaming through its thatch. As he watched this, uncertain what to do, an old bent Dorobo woman came through the doorway carrying a chopper and began to cut herself some wood from the dead boughs that lay about the clearing. As she worked she grumbled to herself.

"Eh! Eh! What it is to be old and have no grandson to cut wood for his grannie!"

Podhu listened to this, and more, for a while, and then, finding nothing dangerous here, he stepped into the clearing. The old woman gave a little scream of fright and surprise.

"I'll cut the wood, Mother," said Podhu, and he took the chopper from her hand, laid aside his spear, and set about it. In ten minutes he had a fine pile, and taking an armful, he carried it to the door of the hut.

"May I enter your house, Mother?" he asked, for among Podhu's people, as among others, one does not walk into strange houses without asking.

The old woman had got over her fright and had seated herself upon a log to watch him work. Now she gave a cackle of laughter.

"Eh!" she babbled. "A fine young man. The first I've seen for many a long year. And what are you doing here, all alone so far from your friends, eh? Asking to go into my house! How do you know I'm not a witch, young man? How do you know that once you're in my house I shan't turn you into an ape, or a snake, or a little crawling lizard, eh?"

"Mother," said Podhu, "I'm tired and I'm lost. I don't think you're a witch, for I listened to you before you saw me, and if you had been one I think you would have known I was there. You only sounded like an old woman who needed the help of a strong grandson. I'll tell you why I'm here, but first let me go in and put down this wood and sit by the fire, for I've not seen one for two days."

Then they went into the house and mended the fire and the old woman shared her meal with Podhu and afterward he told her his story. She listened, nodding her head at the important places, and when he had done she said:

"Ah, but you're a bold young man to come to such a dangerous place as this on such an errand. Perhaps I will help you and perhaps I won't. Perhaps I *can* help you and perhaps I can't. We'll see. Meanwhile let's find out what sort of a grandson you make. You stop here and chop the wood until I make up my mind."

So Podhu lived with the old Dorobo woman, and what a time she gave him! Up in the morning at the crack of dawn, fetching water from the stream, gathering roots, hoeing her little patch of vegetables, chopping wood. That little fire of hers burned more wood than a family of charcoal burners. He chopped wood every minute of the day that he was not doing the other tasks she demanded. And all day long her scolding banged about his ears.

"Eh! What a grandson! Lazy, worthless, idle, graceless! Fit for nothing but polishing the seat of a stool! Podhu! Wood! You haven't brought the wood and the fire's almost out. Eh!"

Every evening he asked her, "Mother, are you going to help me get Aruwa's spear?" And she answered, "What? What's that he says? Spear? Ah, we'll see about that. We'll see."

When he had worked a month for her and was in despair, suddenly, one afternoon, she smiled and told him to stop what he was doing and come and sit beside her.

"Now listen, my son," she said. "Perhaps you think that you've wasted your time here, but that's not true. We Dorobo know the Elephant Folk, and we know that a man must have three things if he is to succeed with them. He must have courage and that you have or you would not be here. He must have also patience and goodness, and that I had to find out. Even with these it will be dangerous to speak with them, for you have injured one and they do not easily forget that. But I'll give you something that may help a little and after that you must just trust to your luck."

Then from underneath the skin she wore, the old Dorobo woman took a small blue bead as big as a bean. It glowed like a piece of sky, and when she placed it on Podhu's open hand he could see into it but not through it.

"That, my son, is a magic bead. Our hunters carry it when they hunt the elephant, and if they are good and patient and brave then *sometimes* the elephants do what they wish them to. Tomorrow I will show you the path that leads to the kraal of the Elephant Folk and you must take your chance or go home without your brother's spear."

Early next morning the old Dorobo woman took Podhu to a small track that left the clearing. "Follow this," she said. "Where it divides, take the bigger; where it becomes three, take the middle one. In perhaps four hours you will come to the kraal of the Elephant Folk. Leave your spear and everything that you carry or wear except the bead and go round the kraal wall until you find the entrance. Then enter boldly and stand where they can see you, with your eyes to the ground. Don't speak until you are spoken to and then, if they don't kill you first, you must speak up boldly and ask for what you want."

Then Podhu thanked her and followed the track. And where it divided he took the bigger and where it spread into three he took the middle. He went as silently as he was able, and the trees about him seemed to get bigger and older and more twisted until suddenly, after four hours, the path stopped at the foot of an immense wall of uprooted trees piled and flung higgledy-piggledy one on top of the other.

This must be the hedge of the elephants' kraal, he thought, and looking to right and left he saw that this wall of branches and trunks and creepers curved away through the trees on either side. Podhu turned along a small path that followed the hedge until he saw before him a wide road beaten out of the forest by many huge feet. He saw that this road ran through a gap in the kraal wall and he judged that this was the entrance. Then, remembering the old Dorobo woman's advice, he laid his spear and skin bag and the skin he wore and the necklace round his neck all on the ground; and, taking only the blue bead, he stepped naked into the road, and with his heart thumping in his chest, he walked slowly through the entrance.

Before him was a vast expanse of beaten earth many times greater than the biggest field Podhu had ever seen. There seemed to be only the entrance he had come through, for the great hedge curled right round him and the trees outside this hung over, their branches giving shade. In this were hundreds and hundreds of elephants, more than Podhu had imagined to be in the whole world. All kinds of elephants, old and young, great bulls with polished white tusks, wrinkled cows fussing over calves which stood between their legs. All about him ears flapped, heads tossed, tails twisted, and black trunks swung. One great fig tree stood within the hedge on the far side of the kraal and beneath this rested a gigantic old bull as big as a hill, so old that his skin hung in folds, his tusks so heavy that his head hung down with the weight of them. This Podhu judged to be the chief, and marking his position, Podhu bent his head and walked unsteadily toward him, panting through dry lips.

When first he had entered there had come a silence over the elephants, then all about him Podhu heard them stirring like rocks rumbling down a hillside. The deep grumbling in a thousand throats turned to a roar of anger and a young bull screamed, "Kill him! It's the man who threw the spear."

By the time that Podhu stopped in front of the chief (he could only see his feet for he kept his head bent), he knew, although no one had touched him, that they were all pressing close, and he could feel the ground trembling as they rolled forward. Or perhaps it was his own trembling. He stood still waiting to be killed, and then the noise about him grew less and at last there was nothing except for a monstrous breathing.

It seemed to Podhu that he stood like this for a long time, a small, naked, shivering Podhu. Then he heard a thin tired voice that somehow *sounded* gray. It was the old chief and he might have been speaking to himself.

"A man," he said gently. "An animal who walks more upright than an ape, looking like a forked stick. A creature without mercy or pity. Of all living things why have *you* come here?"

Podhu was so surprised that he forgot to be afraid. He had never thought of himself as being like that. He looked up at the old bull and spoke up boldly so that all could hear.

"Elephant Folk, when you came to graze in my garden I was unkind to you. I took my brother's spear and threw it, and by ill luck it struck one of you who took it with him back to the forest. My brother now says that I must give him back his spear, or he will kill me. That is why I have come here. Either give me back my spear, or kill me as I deserve."

When he had finished his speech there was a long silence, and then all the elephants began to talk at once until they realized that their chief was speaking. Then immediately they were quiet.

". . . my brothers . . ." he was saying. "We must not behave like this, or our visitor here will mistake us for men."

The elephants shuffled their feet on the beaten mud (they rasped like giant files on wood), and grumbled.

"My friend," said the old bull to Podhu, "I think that you had better leave us for a little while so that we may decide what shall be done with you."

Then two elephants led Podhu away across the kraal and allowed him to sit in the shade while the rest called a meeting. The discussion was long and excited. Podhu could hear one or more of them trumpeting from where he sat with his two guards, but at last all grew still, and he realized that they had made up their minds about him. He was led back to the council and the old bull spoke again.

"Young man," he said, "if we have your brother's spear, we will give it to you because you are brave and because we like your impudence in coming here. But first you must promise us two things."

Podhu, whose heart had begun to sing with relief, became serious again.

"First, you must teach your sons to build little huts beside your growing maize. And in those huts, in each field, a child shall sit and watch. Then when we Elephant Folk come to eat, the child shall run out and bang an iron pot, and when we hear that we shall go away and leave the crop alone. How else can we tell what is yours by planting and what is ours since it grows by nature?"

"That I'll do," said Podhu (and so he did, for always now in Africa a child watches the ripening maize and the animals will usually respect the clatter of his beaten pot).

"Next," went on the chief, "you must promise not to tell anyone the way to this place."

"That I'll do willingly," said Podhu (and no one has ever again found the elephants' kraal, as they would have done if Podhu had broken his promise).

Then they led him round behind the fig tree, and there, stacked in rows, were hundreds of spears that had been brought by the elephants and, among them, Podhu's eager eye at once saw Old Ramogi's magic spear. He took it, and bowing low to the old bull, he thanked them all for their kindness and went away.

He collected the things he had left beside the kraal hedge and began his journey home. He meant to thank the old Dorobo woman who had helped him, but he could never again find the clearing where she lived, and sometimes he wondered if she *had* been a witch after all, for not all witches are wicked. But indeed on that journey he became so thoroughly lost that he wandered for three days before he found his way out of the forest and back to his home.

There all his people came running to meet him and he waved Aruwa's spear on high and Aruwa took it with shining eyes, he was so happy to get it back. He was in fact so pleased that he forgot to thank Podhu.

Then everyone asked questions and Podhu told his story (he was, of course, careful to say nothing that would betray the elephants' kraal) and when he reached the end he took out the blue bead and showed it to them all.

Everyone gasped at its beauty. It glowed more wonderfully than ever in that sunny place, and it passed from hand to hand with exclamations of admiration and wonder. Down the line of women it went, who handled it enviously and parted with it slowly, until it reached the children. They hardly dared touch such a magic thing and passed it on quickly until it reached the hands of Aruwa's smallest son, whose name was Onyango. And Onyango, who was not old enough to know better, popped it into his mouth and swallowed it.

Consternation!

When they realized what had happened you never heard such a row. Everyone shouted advice. Podhu's wife (who fancied wearing that bead) screamed and picked up little Onyango by the heels and thumped him on the back. Onyango yelled. Aruwa's wife thought her son was being killed and attacked her sister (the brothers had married sisters, you will remember) and pulled her hair. Three cooking pots were broken and an old servant of Aruwa's fell in the fire and had to be sat in the stream to put him out. He wasn't hurt and no one was very sorry for him because he was always doing it to attract attention.

But the bead was inside little Onyango and there it stayed.

Then Podhu, who was gray with anger, said to Aruwa, "My brother, when I lost your magic spear you said that

I must get it back or you would kill me. Then when I risked my life with the elephants and did get it back you failed to thank me. Now, Brother, I think that the stick is about another back. Your son has swallowed my magic bead. What are you going to do about it?"

Aruwa answered, "Brother, before we came here I mentioned the saying of our people that it is easier for cats and dogs to live together without quarreling than it is for brothers. We have between us showed that to be a true saying. Tomorrow, I will move to another place and make my village alone, like the rest of our brothers."

"I think that will be best," said Podhu, "but Onyango, your son, must stay with me as my son, for he has my magic bead."

Then Aruwa bowed his head, for he loved his son but admitted the justice of what Podhu said.

And so it was done and afterward the brothers lived apart and there were no more quarrels. As for Onyango, he stayed with his new father, Podhu, and didn't mind a bit after the first few days, for Podhu loved him also. But he got a new name, for always afterward he was known as Onyango Who Has the Bead.

And so far as I know he has it still.

LENNY'S RED-LETTER DAY

Bernard Ashley

Lenny Fraser is a boy in my class. Well, he's a boy in my class when he comes. But to tell the truth, he doesn't come very often. He stays away from school for a week at a time, and I'll tell you where he is. He's at the shops, stealing things sometimes, but mainly just opening the doors for people. He does it to keep himself warm. I've seen him in our shop. When he opens the door for someone, he stands around inside till he gets sent out. Of course, it's quite warm enough in school, but he hates coming. He's always got long, tangled hair, not very clean, and his clothes are too big or too small, and they call him "Fleabag." He sits at a desk without a partner, and no one wants to hold his hand in games. All right, they're not to blame; but he isn't, either. His mother never gets up in the morning, and his house is dirty. It's a house that everybody runs past very quickly.

41

But Lenny makes me laugh a lot. In the playground, he's always saying funny things out of the corner of his mouth. He doesn't smile when he does it. He says these funny things as if he's complaining. For example, when Mr. Cox the deputy head came to school in his new car, Lenny came too, that day; but he didn't join in all the admiration. He looked at the little car and said to me, "Anyone missing a skateboard?"

He misses all the really good things, though—the School Journeys and the outing. And it was a big shame about his birthday.

It happens like this with birthdays in our class. Miss Blake lets everyone bring their cards and perhaps a small present to show the others. Then everyone sings "Happy Birthday" and we give them bumps in the playground. If people can't bring a present, they tell everyone what they've got instead. I happen to know some people make up the things that they've got just to be up with the others, but Miss Blake says it's good to share our Red-Letter Days.

I didn't know about these Red-Letter Days before. I thought they were something special in the post, like my dad handles in his Post Office in the shop. But Miss Blake told us they are red printed words in the prayer books, meaning special days.

Well, what I'm telling you is that Lenny came to school on his birthday this year. Of course, he didn't tell us it was his birthday, and, as it all worked out, it would have been better if Miss Blake hadn't noticed it in the

42

register. But, "How nice!" she said. "Lenny's here on his birthday, and we can share it with him."

It wasn't very nice for Lenny. He didn't have any cards to show the class, and he couldn't think of a birthday present to tell us about. He couldn't even think of anything funny to say out of the corner of his mouth. He just had to stand there looking foolish until Miss Blake started the singing of "Happy Birthday"—and then half the people didn't bother to sing it. I felt very sorry for him, I can tell you. But that wasn't the worst. The worst happened in the playground. I went to take his head end for bumps, and no one would come and take his feet. They all walked away. I had to finish up just patting him on the head with my hands, and before I knew what was coming out I was telling him, "You can come home to tea with me, for your birthday." And he said, yes, he would come.

My father works very hard in the Post Office, in a corner of our shop; and my mother stands at the door all day, where people pay for their groceries. When I get home from school, I carry cardboard boxes out to the yard and jump on them, or my big sister Nalini shows me which shelves to fill and I fill them with jam or chapatis—or birthday cards. On this day, though, I thought I'd use my key and go in through the side door and take Lenny straight upstairs—then hurry down again and tell my mum and dad that I'd got a friend in for an hour. I thought, I can get a birthday card and some cake and ice cream from the shop, and Lenny can go home

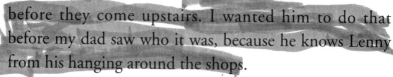

before they come upstairs. I wanted him to do that before my dad saw who it was, because he knows Lenny from his hanging around the shops.

Lenny said some funny things on the way home from school, but you know, I couldn't relax and enjoy them properly. I felt ashamed because I was wishing all the time that I hadn't asked him to come home with me. The bottoms of his trousers dragged along the ground, he had no buttons on his shirt so the sleeves flapped, and his hair must have made it hard for him to see where he was going.

I was in luck because the shop was very busy. My dad had a queue of people to pay out, and my mum had a crowd at the till. I left Lenny in the living room and I went down to get what I wanted from the shop. I found him a birthday card with a badge in it. When I came back, he was sitting in a chair and the television was switched on. He's a good one at helping himself, I thought. We watched some cartoons and then we played Monopoly, which Lenny had seen on the shelf. We had some crisps and cakes and lemonade while we were playing; but I had only one eye on my Monopoly moves—the other eye was on the clock all the time. I was getting very impatient for the game to finish, because it looked as if Lenny would still be there when they came up from the shop. I did some really bad moves so that I could lose quickly, but it's very difficult to hurry up Monopoly, as you may know.

In the end I did such stupid things—like buying too many houses and selling Park Lane and Mayfair—that he won the game. He must have noticed what I was doing, but he didn't say anything to me. Hurriedly, I gave him his birthday card. He pretended not to take very much notice of it, but he put it in his shirt, and kept feeling it to make sure it was still there. At least, that's what I thought he was making sure about, there inside his shirt.

It was just the right time to say goodbye, and I'm just thinking he can go without anyone seeing him, when my sister came in. She had run up from the shop for something or other, and she put her head inside the room. At some other time, I would have laughed out loud at her stupid face. When she saw Lenny, she looked as if she'd opened the door and seen something really unpleasant. I could gladly have given her a good kick. She shut the door a lot quicker than she opened it, and I felt really bad about it.

"Nice to meet you," Lenny joked, but his face said he wanted to go, too, and I wasn't going to be the one to stop him.

I let him out, and I heaved a big sigh. I felt good about being kind to him, the way you do when you've done a sponsored swim, and I'd done it without my mum and dad frowning at me about who I brought home. Only Nalini had seen him, and everyone knows she can make things seem worse than they are. I washed the glasses, and I can remember singing while I stood at the sink. I was feeling very pleased with myself.

45

My good feeling lasted about fifteen minutes; just long enough to be wearing off slightly. Then Nalini came in again and destroyed it altogether.

"Prakash, have you seen that envelope that was on the television top?" she asked. "I put it on here when I came in from school."

"No," I said. It was very soon to be getting worried, but things inside me were turning over like clothes in a washing machine. I knew already where all this was going to end up. "What was in it?" My voice sounded to me as if it was coming from a great distance.

She was looking everywhere in the room, but she kept coming back to the television top as if the envelope would mysteriously appear there. She stood there now, staring at me. "*What was in it?* What was in it was only a Postal Order for five pounds! Money for my school trip!"

"What does it look like?" I asked, but I think we both knew that I was only stalling. We both knew where it had gone.

"It's a white piece of paper in a brown envelope. It says 'Postal Order' on it, in red."

My washing machine inside nearly went into a fast spin when I heard that. It was certainly Lenny's Red-Letter Day! But how could he be so ungrateful, I thought, when I was the only one to be kind to him? I clenched my fist while I pretended to look around. I wanted to punch him hard on the nose.

Then Nalini said what was in both our minds. "It's that dirty kid who's got it. I'm going down to tell Dad. I don't know what makes you so stupid."

Right at that moment I didn't know what made me so stupid, either, as to leave him up there on his own. I should have known. Didn't Miss Banks once say something about leopards never changing their spots?

When the shop closed, there was an awful business in the room. My dad was shouting-angry at me, and my mum couldn't think of anything good to say.

"You know where this boy lives," my dad said. "Tell me now, while I telephone the police. There's only one way of dealing with this sort of thing. If I go up there, I shall only get a mouthful of abuse. As if it isn't bad enough for you to see me losing things out of the shop, you have to bring untrustworthy people upstairs!"

My mum saw how unhappy I was, and she tried to make things better. "Can't you cancel the Postal Order?" she asked him.

"Of course not. Even if he hasn't had the time to cash it somewhere else by now, how long do you think the Post Office would let me be Sub-Postmaster if I did that sort of thing?"

I was feeling very bad for all of us, but the thought of the police calling at Lenny's house was making me feel worse.

"I'll get it back," I said. "I'll go to his house. It's only along the road from the school. And if I don't get it back, I can get the exact number of where he lives. *Then* you

47

can telephone the police." I had never spoken to my dad
like that before, but I was feeling all shaky inside, and all
the world seemed a different place to me that evening.
I didn't give anybody a chance to argue with me. I ran
straight out of the room and down to the street.

My secret hopes of seeing Lenny before I got to his
house didn't come to anything. All too quickly I was
there, pushing back his broken gate and walking up the
cracked path to his front door. There wasn't a door
knocker. I flapped the letter box, and I started to think
my dad was right. The police would have been better
doing this than me.

I had never seen his mother before, only heard about
her from other kids who lived near. When she opened
the door, I could see she was a small lady with a tight
mouth and eyes that said, "Who are you?" and "Go away
from here!" at the same time.

She opened the door only a little bit, ready to slam it
on me. I had to be quick.

"Is Lenny in, please?" I asked her.

She said, "What's it to you?"

"He's a friend of mine," I told her. "Can I see him,
please?"

She made a face as if she had something nasty in her
mouth. "LENNY!" she shouted. "COME HERE!"

Lenny came slinking down the passage, like one of
those scared animals in a circus. He kept his eyes on her
hands, once he'd seen who it was at the door. There
weren't any funny remarks coming from him.

She jerked her head at me. "How many times have I told you not to bring kids to the house?" she shouted at him. She made it sound as if she was accusing him of a bad crime.

Lenny had nothing to say. She was hanging over him like a vulture about to fix its talons into a rabbit. It looked so out of place that it didn't seem real. Then it came to me that it could be play-acting—the two of them. He had given her the five pounds, and she was putting this on to get rid of me quickly.

But suddenly she slammed the door so hard in my face I could see how the glass in it came to be broken.

"Well, I don't want kids coming to my door!" she shouted at him on the other side. "Breaking the gate, breaking the windows, wearing out the path. How can I keep this place nice when I'm forever dragging to the door?"

She hit him then, I know she did. There was no play-acting about the bang as a foot hit the door, and Lenny yelling out loud as if a desk lid had come down on his head. But I didn't stop to hear any more. I'd heard enough to turn my stomach sick. Poor Lenny—I'd been worried about my mum and dad seeing him—and look what happened when his mother saw me! She had to be mad, that woman. And Lenny had to live with her! I didn't feel like crying, although my eyes had a hot rawness in them. More than anything, I just wanted to be back at home with my own family and the door shut tight.

Seeing my dad's car turn the corner was as if my dearest wish had been granted. He was going slowly, searching for me, with Nalini sitting up in front with big eyes. I waved, and ran to them. I got in the back and I drew in my breath to tell them to go straight home. It was worth fifty pounds not to have them knocking at Lenny's house, never mind five. But they were too busy trying to speak to me.

"Have you been to the house? Did you say anything?"

"Yes, I've been to the house, but—"

"Did you accuse him?"

"No. I didn't have a chance—"

They both sat back in their seats, as if the car would drive itself home.

"Well, we must be grateful for that."

"We found the Postal Order."

I could hardly believe what my ears were hearing. *They had found the Postal Order.* Lenny hadn't taken it, after all!

"It wasn't in its envelope," Nalini was saying. "He must have taken it out of that when he was tempted by it. But we can't accuse him of screwing up an envelope and hiding it in his pocket."

"No, no," I was saying, urging her to get on with things and tell me. "So where was it?"

"In with the Monopoly money. He couldn't put it back on the television, so he must have kept it in his pile of Monopoly money, and put it back in the box."

"Oh."

"Mum found it. In all the commotion after you went out she knocked the box off the chair, and when she picked the bits up, there was the Postal Order."

"It's certainly a good job you said nothing about it," my dad said. "And a good job I didn't telephone the police. We should have looked very small."

All I could think was how small I had just felt, standing at Lenny's slammed door and hearing what his mother had said to him. And what about him getting beaten for having a friend call at his house?

My dad tried to be cheerful. "Anyway, who won?" he asked.

"Lenny won the Monopoly," I said.

In bed that night, I lay awake a long time, thinking about it all. Lenny had taken some hard punishment from his mother. Some Red-Letter Day it had turned out to be! He would bear some hard thoughts about Prakash Patel.

He didn't come to school for a long time after that. But when he did, my heart sank into my boots. He came straight across the playground, the same flappy sleeves and dragging trouser bottoms, the same long, tangled hair—and he came straight for me. What would he do? Hit me? Spit in my face?

As he got close, I saw what was on his shirt, pinned there like a medal. It was his birthday badge.

"It's a good game, that Monopoly," he said out of the corner of his mouth. It was as if he was trying to tell me something.

51

"Yes," I said. "It's a good game all right."

I hadn't got the guts to tell him that I'd gone straight home that night and thrown it in the dustbin. Dealings with houses didn't appeal to me anymore.

BARBIE

Gary Soto

The day after Christmas, Veronica Solis and her baby sister, Yolanda, nestled together on the couch to watch the morning cartoons. Bumbling Inspector Gadget was in trouble again, unaware that the edge of the cliff was crumbling under his feet. Soon he was sliding down the mountain toward a pit of alligators. He commanded, "Go, go, gadget umbrella," and a red umbrella popped out of his hat. He landed safely just a few feet from a dark green alligator and dusted himself off.

Veronica liked this show, but she was really waiting for the next one: "My Little Pony." That show had lots of Barbie commercials and Veronica was in love with Barbie, her blond hair, her slim waist and long legs, and the glamorous clothes on tiny hangers. She had wanted a Barbie for as long as she could remember and almost got one last Christmas, but her Uncle Rudy, who had more money than all her other uncles combined, bought her the worst kind of doll, an imitation Barbie.

Veronica had torn the silver wrapping off her gift and found a black-haired doll with a flat, common nose, not like Barbie's cute, upturned nose. She had wanted to cry, but she gave her uncle a hug, forced a smile, and went to her bedroom to stare at the doll. A tear slid down her cheek.

"You ugly thing," she snapped and threw the imposter against the wall. The doll lay on the floor, eyes open like the dead. Immediately, Veronica felt ashamed. She picked up the doll and set it beside her.

"I'm sorry. I don't hate you," she whispered. "It's just that you're not a *real* Barbie." She noticed that the forehead was chipped where it had struck the wall, and that one of the eyelashes was peeling off like a scab.

"Oh, no," she gasped. Veronica tried to push the eyelash back into place, but it came off and stuck to her thumb. "Doggone it," she mumbled and returned to the living room, where her uncle was singing Mexican Christmas songs.

He stopped to sip from his coffee cup and pat Veronica's hand. "Did you name your doll yet?"

"No, not yet." Veronica looked at the floor. She hoped that he wouldn't ask her to bring it out.

"Let's see her. I'll sing her a song," he teased.

Veronica didn't want him to see that the doll's face was chipped and one of her eyelashes was gone.

"She's asleep," she said.

"Well, in that case, we'll let her sleep," he said. "I'll sing her a lullaby, 'Rock-a-Bye Baby' in Spanish."

That was last year. There had been no Barbie this Christmas either. Today was just a cold, winter morning in front of the television.

Her Uncle Rudy came over to the house with his girlfriend, Donna. Veronica's mother was uneasy. Why was the girlfriend here? Was this the moment? She dried her hands on a kitchen towel and told the children to go play outside. She turned to the woman and, ignoring her brother, asked, "What'd you get for Christmas?"

"A robe and slippers," she said, looking at Rudy, then added, "and a sweatsuit from my brother."

"Come, have a seat. I'll start coffee."

"Helen, would you call Veronica back inside?" Rudy asked. "We have an extra present for her."

"OK," she said, hurrying to the kitchen, her face worried because something was up and it could be marriage. She called, "Veronica, your uncle wants you."

Veronica dropped her end of the jump rope, leaving her sister and brother to carry on without her. She walked back into the house and stood by her uncle; but she couldn't take her eyes off the woman.

"How's school?" asked her uncle.

"Fine," she said shyly.

"Getting good grades?"

"Pretty good."

"As good as the boys? Better?"

"Lots better."

"Any *novios*?"

Donna slapped Rudy's arm playfully. "Rudy, quit teasing the child. Give it to her."

"OK," he said, patting Donna's hand. He turned to Veronica. "I have something for you. Something I know you wanted."

Uncle Rudy's girlfriend reached in a package at her feet and brought out a Barbie doll in a striped, one-piece swimsuit. "This is for you, honey."

Veronica stared at the woman, then at the doll. The woman's eyes were almost as blue, and her hair almost as blond as Barbie's. Veronica slowly took the Barbie from the woman and very softly said, "Thank you." She gave her uncle a big hug, taking care not to smash Barbie against his chest. Veronica smiled at the woman, then at her mother, who returned from the kitchen with a pot of coffee and a plate of powdery-white donuts.

"Look, Mom, a Barbie," Veronica said happily.

"Oh, Rudy, you're spoiling this girl," Mrs. Solis chided.

"And that's not all," Rudy said. "Donna, show her the clothes."

The woman brought out three outfits: a summer dress, a pants suit, and a lacy gown the color of mother-of-pearl.

"They're lovely!" said the mother. She held the summer dress up and laughed at how tiny it was.

"I like them a lot," said Veronica. "It's just like on TV."

The grownups sipped their coffee and watched Veronica inspect the clothes. After a few minutes Rudy sat up and cleared his throat.

"I have something to say," he said to his sister, who already suspected what it was. "We're getting married—soon."

He patted Donna's hand, which sported a sparkling ring, and announced a second time that he and Donna were getting married. The date wasn't set yet, but they would have their wedding in the spring. Veronica's mother, feigning surprise, lifted her eyes and said, "Oh, how wonderful! Oh, Rudy—and Donna." She kissed her brother and the woman.

"Did you hear, Veronica? Your uncle is going to get married." She hesitated, then added, "To Donna."

Veronica pretended to look happy, but she was too preoccupied with her new doll.

In her bedroom Veronica hugged her Barbie and told her she was beautiful. She combed Barbie's hair with a tiny blue comb and dressed her in the three outfits. She made believe that Barbie was on a lunch date with a girlfriend from work, the fake Barbie with the chipped forehead and missing eyelash.

"Oh, look—boys!" the ugly doll said. "They're so cute."

"Oh, those boys," Barbie said coolly. "They're OK, but Ken is so much more handsome. And richer."

"They're good-looking to me. I'm not as pretty as you, Barbie."

"That's true," Barbie said. "But I still like you. How's your sandwich?"

"Good, but not as good as your sandwich," the ugly doll answered.

Veronica was eager to make Barbie the happiest person in the world. She dressed her in her swimsuit and said in a fake English accent, "You look smashing, my child."

"And who are you going to marry?" the fake Barbie asked.

"The king," she announced. Veronica raised Barbie's movable arms. "The king is going to buy me a yacht and build me a swimming pool." Veronica made Barbie dive into an imaginary pool. "The king loves me more than money. He would die for me."

Veronica played in her room all afternoon, and the next day called her friend Martha. Martha had two Barbies and one Ken. She invited Veronica to come over to play Barbies, and play they did. The three Barbies went to Disneyland and Magic Mountain and ate at an expensive restaurant where they talked about boys. Then all three took turns kissing Ken.

"Ken, you kiss too hard," Martha giggled.

"You forgot to shave," whined Veronica.

"Sorry," Ken said.

"That's better," they said, laughing, and clacked the dolls' faces together.

But at the end of the day the two girls got into an argument when Martha tried to switch the Barbies so she would get Veronica's newer Barbie. Veronica saw that

Martha was trying to trick her and pushed her against the bureau, yelling, "You stupid cheater!" She left with her three outfits and Barbie under her arm.

At the corner she hugged and kissed Barbie. "That's the last time we're going to her house," said Veronica. "She almost stole you."

She sat on the curb, dressed Barbie in her pants suit, then walked through an alley where she knew there was an orange tree. She stopped under the tree, which was heavy with oranges the size of softballs, and swiped one.

As she walked home she peeled the orange with her polish-chipped nails and looked around the neighborhood. With her Barbie doll pressed under her arm, she was happy. The day was almost over, and soon she and Barbie would be sitting down to dinner. After she finished the orange, she wiped her hands on her pants and started to play with Barbie.

"Oh, it's a beautiful day to look pretty," Barbie said. "Yes, I'm going to—"

Veronica stopped in midsentence. Barbie's head was gone. Veronica waved her hand over the space where a smile and blond hair had been only a few minutes ago.

"Darn it," she hissed. "Her head's gone."

She fell to one knee and felt around. She picked up ragged leaves, loose dirt, and bottle caps. "Where is it?" She checked the leaf-choked gutter and raked her hand through the weeds along a fence. She slowly retraced her steps into the alley, desperately scanning the ground. She looked at the headless Barbie in her hand. She wanted to cry but knew it would just make her eyes blurry.

"Where are you?" Veronica called to the head. "Please let me find you."

She came to the orange tree. She got down and searched on all fours, but found nothing. She pounded the ground with her fists and burst into tears.

"She's ruined," Veronica sobbed. "Oh, Barbie, look at you. You're no good anymore." She looked through her tears at Barbie and got mad. How could Barbie do this to her after only one day?

For the next hour she searched the street and the alley. She even knocked on Martha's door and asked her if she had seen Barbie's head.

"No," Martha said. She kept the door half-closed because she was afraid that Veronica was still mad at her for trying to switch their Barbies. "Did you lose it?"

"It just fell off. I don't know what happened. It was brand-new."

"How did it fall off?"

"How do I know? It just fell off. Stupid thing!"

Veronica looked so distressed that Martha went outside and helped her look, assuring Veronica that together they would find the head.

"One time I lost my bike keys at the playground," Martha said. "I just looked and looked. I just got on my knees and crawled around. Nobody helped me. I found them all by myself."

Veronica ignored Martha's chatter. She was busy parting weeds with her hands and overturning rocks and boards under which the head might have rolled. After a while Veronica had a hard time concentrating and had to keep reminding herself what she was looking for. "Head," she said, "look for the head." But everything became jumbled together. She stared at the ground so long that she couldn't tell an eggshell from a splintered squirt gun.

If only it could talk, wished Veronica, who was once again on the verge of tears. If only it could yell, "Over here, I'm here by the fence. Come and get me." She blamed herself, then Martha. If they hadn't had that argument, everything would have been all right. She would have played and then returned home. She probably jinxed her Barbie when she pushed Martha against the chest of drawers. Maybe that was when Barbie's head had come loose; she had been holding Barbie while she fought Martha.

When it began to get dark Martha said she had to go. "But I'll help you tomorrow if you want," she said.

Veronica puckered her mouth and shouted, "It's all your fault! You made me mad. You tried to cheat me. My Barbie was more beautiful than yours, and now see what you've done!" She held the headless Barbie up for Martha to see. Martha turned away and ran.

That night Veronica sat in her room. She felt that she had betrayed Barbie by not caring for her and couldn't stand to look at her. She wanted to tell her mother, but she knew Mom would scold her for being a *mensa*.

"If only I could tell Uncle Rudy's girlfriend," she said. "She would understand. She would do something."

Finally, Veronica dressed in her nightie, brushed her teeth, and jumped into bed. She started reading a library book about a girl in New York City who had lost her cat, but tossed it aside because the words on the page meant nothing. It was a made-up story, while her own sadness was real.

"I shouldn't have gone," said Veronica, staring at the ceiling. "I should have stayed home and played by myself."

She sat up and tried to read again, but she couldn't concentrate. She picked at a scab on her wrist and tried to lull herself to sleep with sad thoughts. When she couldn't stand it anymore, she kicked off the blankets and walked over to her Barbie, which lay on a chest of drawers. She picked up the fake Barbie, too.

"Let's go to sleep," she whispered to both dolls, and carried them lovingly to bed.

GHOST CAT

Donna Hill

Ⅰt was growing so dark that Filmore had to stop reading; but as soon as he put his book down, he began to notice the loneliness again.

His mother had been driving without a word ever since they had turned onto this remote and bumpy road. Jodi was asleep, curled up in back with her stuffed animal friend. There was nothing to see out the window except black trees and shrubs along the roadside thrashing in the wind. To the west, through the trees, he could see that the sun had melted onto the horizon, but to the east the sky looked dark and bruised.

Suddenly his mother said, "That must be the house." She stopped the car.

Jodi sat up. "Are we here?" Jodi always awoke at once, alert and happy. She did not seem to know what loneliness and sorrow were. Jodi had glossy black curls and eyes like agates. She was little for her six years, but sturdy and fearless, as even Filmore would admit, but only to himself. To others, sometimes as a compliment, he said she was daft.

"You two wait here while I take a look," said their mother.

Filmore watched their mother walk along the path between the swaying, overgrown bushes. She looked small, walking alone, not much taller than his sister, in fact. Filmore whispered, "Jodi, don't you wish Daddy were here with us?"

Jodi was brushing down the apron of her animal friend.

"Remember last summer with Daddy?" Filmore said. "The beach, how broad and clean and dazzling it was? Remember what fun we had in the boat?"

Jodi turned her animal friend about, inspecting her from all sides.

"Here comes mother," Filmore said. "Let's not remind her of Daddy." But he needn't have warned Jodi. She seemed not to have heard a word.

"This is it," their mother said. "Help me with the bags, please, Filmore."

He and Jodi scrambled out of the car.

"Wait, wait!" Jodi called. "I dropped Mrs. Tiggy-winkle! Don't worry, Mrs. Tiggy-winkle! We'll never leave you! We love you!"

"What does she care," Filmore protested. For some reason he was annoyed with his sister. "She's only a stuffed hedgehog."

"She is not! She's a raccoon!"

"Listen, either she's a hedgehog or she's not Mrs. Tiggy-winkle!"

"Filmore, please," their mother said, pushing through the creaking gate.

A stone path led to a cottage perched on a little bluff overlooking the cove. Trees were sighing and moaning over the roof, and shrubs whispered at the door. The wind dropped suddenly as though the house were holding its breath, and Filmore could hear the push of waves up the beach and their scraping retreat over pebbles and shells.

His mother paused at the stoop to search through her bag for the key. Now Filmore could see scaling paint, shutters hanging loose, and windows opaque with dust. "What a dump!" he muttered.

When he saw his mother's face, he was sorry. His mother had gone back to teaching and labored to keep up their home; no one knew better than Filmore how hard it had been.

"The agent told us we'd have to take it as is," she said. "That's how we can afford it." She found the key, but could hardly shove the door open for sand that had sucked up against it.

"We came for the beach, anyway," Filmore said. "Who cares about the house! I wouldn't care if it was haunted!"

"Oh, I love the haunted house!" Jodi cried, bursting into the front room. "Oh, we have a big window with the whole black sky in it! Oh, and a fireplace! And rocking

65

chairs!" The floor squealed under her feet as she ran around excitedly. "And here's the kitchen, with a black monster stove!"

Their mother laughed. She had the same dark curly hair, the same eyes as Jodi, and when she laughed, she did not look much older. "It's charming, really. Just needs a little work. But first we need some sleep."

They climbed narrow stairs and opened creaking doors to three small rooms with beds under dust covers. The covers pleased their mother and made Jodi laugh. "Ghosts and more ghosts!" she cried.

In his unfamiliar little room above the kitchen, Filmore kept waking in the night to whistles, squeals, and thumps that could have been ghosts in the house, that could have been anything sinister at all.

The next morning, Filmore woke to the melancholy crying of gulls. When he heard Jodi's light voice below, he pulled his clothes on hurriedly and went down to the kitchen.

"Good morning, dear," his mother said from the stove, where she was already cooking breakfast. "Did you sleep well?"

"I didn't sleep at all," Jodi put in cheerfully. "Neither did Mrs. Tiggy-winkle. We stayed awake all night and listened to the haunted house."

Filmore did not want to admit his own feelings. "You're daft!"

"Something is here, you know," Jodi insisted. "Something besides us!"

"And I know what it is." Their mother laughed. "Sand! We'll get rid of it right now."

The house was so small that sweeping and dusting upstairs and down did not take long, and still there was time for the beach before lunch.

To Filmore, the beach was even more disappointing than the house. It was narrow and deserted, with low, dispirited waves the color of mud as far as the eye could see. There were no houses in sight, just cliffs and scraggy pine trees at each end of the cove. Edging the sand were patches of weeds and damp brown rags of algae that smelled like vinegar. The stain that marked high tide was littered with broken shells, sticks like bones, and here and there a dead fish. A troupe of sandpipers ran up the beach and back, as though frantic to escape.

Jodi loved everything. She made up a joyful beach song as she built a sand dragon and then she pressed Filmore to go with her while she filled her bucket with shells and treasures.

Stumping along at her heels, Filmore demanded, "Why don't you ever talk about Daddy? You were his dear rabbit, don't forget!"

"Look, Filmore!" Jodi cried. "I found a sand dollar!"

After lunch, they drove out for supplies. "It will be fun to see the village and the shops," their mother said.

The village turned out to be only a few houses scattered along the road, and on the beach, one rowboat upside down beside a shack with a sign for bait. The shops were only Judson's General Store and Judson's Gas Station.

A bell jangled as they went into the store. It was dim and cluttered and smelled of dusty bolts of cloth and strong cheese. Behind the counter stood a tall, thin woman who kept her hands in her apron pockets while she looked them over with stern interest.

"Good morning!" their mother said. "I'm Mrs. Coyne. This is my son, Filmore, and my daughter, Jodi. We've rented the Hogarth place."

"Heard you did," said the storekeeper.

"We need milk and a few groceries. Also lumber and nails, if you have them. We'd like to mend the front stoop. You don't think the owner would mind, do you?"

"Not likely. He hasn't seen the place in years. But I'd wait if I were you. See if you like it there, first."

"Don't you think we'll like it?" Filmore asked.

"Been a lot of folks in and out the Hogarth place. City folks, mostly. Like you. They never stay long."

"Because it's rundown, or is there something else?" Filmore asked.

His mother interposed. "Do you happen to know if the chimney works?"

"Did once. Likely needs sweeping."

"Is there someone who might do it for us?"

"Mr. Judson. My husband. He can fix the front stoop, too, if you want. Rehang those shutters. Trim the bushes. You would have to pay, though. The real estate agency won't. Cost you twenty dollars."

"That would be just fine!"

When Mrs. Judson was adding up the prices on a paper bag, Filmore asked, "Why don't people stay long at Hogarth's?"

Mrs. Judson was busy checking her figures.

"Because of what's there besides us," Jodi said. "Isn't that right, Mrs. Judson?"

Their mother looked at Mrs. Judson with a smile, but Mrs. Judson was busy packing groceries.

"But we like it, Mrs. Tiggy-winkle and I. It sounds so beautiful and sad. Especially the little bell."

"What little bell?" Filmore asked.

"Didn't you hear it? It was so sweet last night, going tinkle-clink all around the house."

Mrs. Judson rang up the money with a loud jangle of her register. "Suit you if Mr. Judson comes tomorrow morning?"

Back in the car, Filmore said, "She wasn't very friendly."

"I thought she was," said their mother. "She tried to help us all she could."

"She didn't smile, not once," Filmore said. "And she wouldn't tell us anything."

"That's because she was nervous," Jodi said.

"Why would she be nervous?" their mother asked.

"For us. She thinks we might be afraid in the house."

"But there's nothing to be afraid of!" said their mother.

Jodi laughed. "We know that!"

Early next morning, Mr. Judson arrived in a truck, with toolbox and planks of wood. He too was tall and thin, with the same gaunt face as his wife, but with a tuft of gray beard attached.

All morning while they were on the beach, Filmore could hear Mr. Judson hammering, thumping, and snipping. At noon he came and said, "Chimney's working. I laid a fire. Got to go, now. The missus will be waiting."

They walked with him to his truck. "How do you folks like it here?" he asked, lifting his toolbox into the back.

"We love it!" Jodi answered.

"It's a charming house, really," their mother said. "I wonder why it hasn't been sold?"

"Because of what's here," Jodi said. "Isn't that right, Mr. Judson?"

Mr. Judson was searching among his tools. "Must have left my pliers somewhere, Mrs. Coyne."

"It's a cat," Jodi said.

"A cat, Jodi?" their mother asked. "Are you sure? Is there a cat, Mr. Judson?"

"Never saw one here, myself. Leastwise not in years."

"You mean there used to be a cat?" Filmore asked.

"Mrs. Hogarth, she had one. Hogarth, he moved away when his missus died. Don't know what became of the cat."

"Could it be a neighbor's cat?"

"She has a squeaky little voice," Jodi said. "Probably hoarse from crying."

70

"Haven't heard tell of any lost cats," Mr. Judson said. He went around to the cab of his truck.

"Could it be a stray?"

"Oh, she's not a stray," Jodi said. "She wears a little rusty bell that goes tinkle-clink when she runs. It's so sweet."

Mr. Judson climbed into his truck and turned on the ignition. "If you find my pliers, will you bring them next time?"

As they watched the truck rattle down the road, Filmore asked, "Don't you think the Judsons act strange? Like they're hiding something?"

"No, dear," his mother said. "I think they're just reticent. That's how people are in this part of the country."

That night, Filmore was awakened by someone shaking his toes. "Filmore! I have to tell you something!"

Jodi was leaning against his bed with Mrs. Tiggy-winkle in her arms. Moonlight falling through the window made her eyes like holes in a mask. "Do you hear the cat?" Jodi whispered. "She's prowling and crying all around the house, now. She wants to come in."

Filmore held his breath to listen. He did in fact hear a wailing and sighing and rustling of leaves. "That's the wind."

"And the cat, too," Jodi insisted.

"All right, get in my bed, if you're scared."

"We're not scared. But we are cold." She climbed on the bed and settled the quilt around Mrs. Tiggy-winkle.

71

Filmore rolled over and closed his eyes. "Go to sleep. There isn't any cat. Mr. Judson said so."

"He did not. He said he never saw a cat, leastwise not in years. But we did."

Filmore turned back. "You saw it?"

"Yes, on the beach this afternoon. She was watching us through the weeds, a yellow cat with red eyes."

"Then why haven't mother and I seen it?"

"Because she's invisible."

"You said you saw it!"

"We did! Mrs. Tiggy-winkle and I! Both of us! First we saw her eyes and then we saw her whole self!"

"You don't even know what invisible means!"

"We do too! It means mostly people can't see her."

"It means nobody ever sees her!"

"But she can fix that when she wants to. Anyway, she is prowling and crying right now. She wants somebody to let her in."

"If she's invisible, she can let herself in!" Filmore cried, triumphantly.

"That's not the same," Jodi said, straightening the quilt.

Filmore turned away. "You make me tired! What did you come bothering me for!"

Jodi sighed and threw off the covers.

"You can stay if you're nervous," Filmore muttered.

"We aren't nervous. But you are! So we'll stay."

At breakfast, Jodi said, through a mouthful of blueberry pancakes, "When you have a cat, you're her mother and daddy, you know, so you must never leave her, like Mr. Hogarth did. That's why she's always crying and prowling and never can rest."

Their mother looked down at them from her pancake griddle.

"We have to put some food out for her, Mother," Jodi said.

"If there's any cat around here, it finds its own food," Filmore said.

"That's right, dear. It got along all right before we came."

"No, she didn't! She's skinny all over and her little bones show! Can't I give her my milk? Please, Mother, please!"

Their mother smiled. "Not your milk, Jodi. We'll find some scraps."

Filmore followed Jodi to the kitchen stoop, where she settled the scraps and a pan of water.

"She's already been here, looking for food," Jodi said. "See her paw prints?"

Filmore bent to examine the stoop. "That's just wet sand. The wind did that. You're putting this food here for nothing. No cat's going to eat it."

"Of course not. She's a ghost. Ghosts can't eat."

"Then why are you putting it here!" Filmore exclaimed, exasperated.

"She doesn't need to eat it, just to have it. To know we love her."

On the beach that afternoon, their mother was reading under the umbrella while Jodi sat beside her on the sand, sorting her beach treasure. Filmore waded for a while, but he felt uneasy by himself and soon came back to flop beside his sister.

The grasses above the beach rattled in the wind. "Is the cat watching us now?" he whispered.

"Oh, not now. The hot sand hurts her feet."

"I thought you said she was a ghost!"

"But she can hurt, just the same."

Later, clouds rolled up over the sea and the wind turned cold. Filmore took down the umbrella while his mother folded the beach chair and they ran for the house through pellets of rain.

That evening Filmore forgot the cat in the pleasure of popping corn over a snappy fire. Their mother sat rocking and mending, and Jodi sprawled on the hearth, humming to Mrs. Tiggy-winkle. Firelight threw quivering shadows on the walls. Outside the rain was like handfuls of sand thrown at the windows.

Filmore glanced at his mother. Her face was thoughtful and withdrawn. Whenever he caught her in such a mood, she would quickly smile, as though to insist she was all right. This time, however, she spoke.

"Remember last summer? Our last vacation with Daddy? Remember the day he bought every balloon the man had, and you three went along the beach and gave them away to children? He wanted us to share our happiness. Remember, Jodi, how happy he wanted us to be?"

At "Is it popcorn yet?" Jodi asked. "I don't hear any more pops."

When Filmore passed her the popcorn, she said, "Mrs. Tiggy-winkle feels just the same as me. But not the cat. She hurts. Because she was murdered. That's why she's a ghost."

Filmore saw that his mother's needle had stopped, but she did not look at them.

"When somebody leaves you, they always murder you a little bit. But Mr. Hogarth, he murdered her a lot, until she was dead."

"If you know so much, how did he do it?" Filmore demanded.

"First he starved her and then he drowned her and then he told her she was bad. That's why she's so skinny and wet. She hates to be skinny and wet. She's outside now, crying at the kitchen door. Can't you hear her? She wants to come in by the fire."

"You're daft!" Filmore exclaimed. "That's just the wind!"

"Please, Mother, please! Can't I let her in?"

Their mother gave Filmore a glance that asked for patience. "All right, dear. Let her in."

Jodi rose with Mrs. Tiggy-winkle and went to the kitchen. Filmore heard the kitchen door open and then the screen. A cold draft blew through the room and dashed at the flames on the hearth.

"Hurry up, please!" their mother called. "You're cooling off the house."

When Jodi came back, Filmore said, "Well, where is the cat?"

"She can't come in because she knows you don't love her."

"But you and Mrs. Tiggy-winkle love her! Isn't that enough?"

"Can Mrs. Tiggy-winkle have some more popcorn, please?"

When the fire burned low and their mother announced bedtime, Jodi said, "She's crying again, Mother."

"Jodi, dear, why do you upset yourself this way? Can't you just enjoy your vacation with Filmore and me?"

"Yes, but she has to be happy, too! That's why we came here, you know! Can't I let her sleep on my bed tonight?"

Their mother sighed.

"You think I just imagine her, don't you?"

"Of course!" Filmore said. "You are the only one who sees her!"

"I am not! Mrs. Tiggy-winkle sees her, too!"

"And Mrs. Tiggy-winkle isn't real, either!"

"All right, if I just imagine her, why can't I have her on my bed?"

Their mother smiled. "I can't argue with that."

In his room, Filmore heard the squeal and slap of the screen door and then his sister's clumpy steps on the stairs. Straining, he thought he also heard soft paws running up beside her and the tinkle of a bell.

"Now she's got me doing it!" he muttered.

The rain grew quiet, the wind died, waves gently washed the shore. The next time Filmore opened his eyes, it was nearly daylight. He pulled on his robe and went to his mother's room.

"What is it, Filmore?" she asked. Like Jodi, she always woke up at once.

"Let's see if Jodi really has a cat."

He took her hand as they went down the hall. "You don't believe there's a ghost cat, do you?"

His mother stopped in the hall. "Not literally, dear, of course. But Jodi does, so we must try to be understanding. She's still very little, you know. She isn't quite sure where reality stops and the stories of her mind begin."

"But why would she make up this crazy story?"

"We'll have to see if we can think of why."

Jodi's window opened on a huge dark sea and a rosy horizon. The sound of rolling waves was like the breathing of a giant in sleep. Jodi was curled under the quilt, her black hair shining on the pillow and Mrs. Tiggy-winkle under her chin.

"There's no cat!" Filmore whispered. "She made the whole thing up!" He felt an odd mixture of indignation, relief, and disappointment.

Jodi sat up brightly. "We're not asleep!"

"Did you and Mrs. Tiggy-winkle have a good night?" their mother asked.

"Yes, and so did the ghost cat. She stayed right here on my bed till she got warm and dry, and then she went away."

77

To Filmore she added, "If you don't believe me, look at this! She gave me her bell!"

Jodi opened her hand to show him a little rusty bell on a bit of frayed ribbon.

Filmore was going to accuse her of finding the bell on the beach, when he caught his mother's eye.

"Why did the ghost cat leave you?" their mother asked. "Doesn't she love you?"

"Yes, but she had to go because she was dead. Just like Daddy, you know."

Filmore saw his mother's eyes grow cloudy, but she hid them by hugging Jodi. He went and made a circle with them, turning his face away also.

Muffled by their arms, Jodi said, "That's why we're hugging and crying and smiling, right?"

LUCKY BOY

Philippa Pearce

This was just about a perfect summer afternoon, with sunshine, flowers blooming, and birds singing, even to a cuckoo (only that happened to be Lucy next door, who was good at it); and it was Saturday into the bargain. Everything was in Pat's favour: jobs done, and his family safely in the back garden. He strolled down the front garden to the front gate. Clicked open the gate . . .

Free . . .

And then: "Where are you going, Pat? Will you take me with you, Pat? Take me too, Pat!" The cuckoo had stopped calling, because Lucy had given up mimicry to poke her face between the slats of the dividing fence. "Take me."

If he went through the gate and on, without her, Lucy would bawl. That was understood on both sides. The question was: Would anyone from either house come in response to the bawling? And if they did, would they bother to get to the bottom of things: detain Pat for questioning, cross-examine him on his plans, ruin his perfect afternoon?

Of course, he could run for it—now, instantly. That was perhaps the only certain way of keeping his afternoon to himself. He would just leave Lucy bawling behind him. What made him hesitate was that once he used to take Lucy on expeditions even without her asking. When Lucy had been a baby in a pram, he had helped to wheel her. Later on, when she was old enough to walk, he had taken her to the sweetshop, and he had even shared his pocket money with her. Not so very long ago he had taken her regularly to the swings and the sandpit and seesaw on the Recreation Ground.

So he paused, holding the gate open before him, to reason with her. "I'm not going where I could take you," he said, "you're too little."

But she simply repeated, "Take me."

Pat had delayed, and Lucy's mother must have been watching from the window. She opened the front door and came down the path towards them, carrying a pair of red sandals. She had misunderstood the situation. "Lucy," she said, "you put your sandals on if you're going out of this garden." And then, to Pat, "Are you taking her to the shops or to the swings?"

Pat was going to neither, so he said nothing.

Lucy's mother went straight on, "Because if it's the shops, she can have fourpence."

"No," said Pat. "Not the shops."

"Well, then!" said Lucy's mother to Lucy. "You do as Pat tells you, now." She turned briskly back to the house. Lucy's mother was always like that.

Lucy had been putting on her sandals. Now she went through her front gate, and waited for Pat to come through his. She held out her hand, and he took it.

They walked to the Recreation Ground, towards the swings. The sun still shone, flowers bloomed, birds sang—and Lucy with them; but the afternoon was ruined for Pat.

They were within sight of the swings. "Will you push me high?" Lucy was saying.

He made up his mind then. Instead of loosening his hold of her hand, so that she could run ahead to the swings, he tightened it. He gripped her attention. "Listen, Lucy. We could go somewhere much better than the swings." Yes, he'd take Lucy, rather than not go at all. "We'll go somewhere really exciting—but secret, Lucy, mind. Just you and me, secretly."

"Secretly?"

"Come on."

They veered abruptly from the direction of the swings and scudded along the fencing that bounded the Recreation Ground on its far side. They left behind them the swingers, the sandpit players, and even the football kickers. Down to the lonely end of the Recreation Ground, where Pat had poked about a good deal recently. He had poked about and found a loose fencing stake that could be pried up and swung aside, to make a gap.

"No one's looking. Through here, Lucy—quickly. Squeeze."

Gaps in the fencing of the Recreation Ground were not unheard of; nor boys getting through them when they should not. But trespassing through such holes was disappointing. On the other side of this fence lay only a private garden. True, it ran down to the river; but what was the use of a riverbank neatly turfed and herbaceous bordered and within spying distance of its house? And if one tried to go further along the riverbank, one soon came to another fence, and beyond it, another private garden, and so on. Trespassing boys looked longingly over to the other side of the river, which was open country—thin pasturage, often flooded in winter, with ragged banks grown here and there with willow and alder. They looked, and then they turned back through the gap by which they had come. And in due course the groundsman would notice the hole and stop it up.

Pat's hole had not yet been found by the groundsman, which was a bit of luck; but beyond it, in the garden, lay—yes, *lay* was the very word—the best luck of all.

"Now," Pat said, as Lucy emerged from the hole in the fence into the garden. "Keep down behind the bushes, because of being seen from the house, and follow me. This way to the riverbank; and now—look!"

Lucy gazed, bewildered, awed. The turf of the bank had been mutilated and the flower border smashed by a tangle of boughs and twigs that only yesterday had been the crown of an alder tree, high as a house, that grew on the opposite bank. For years the river had been washing away at the roots of the alder, dislodging a crumb of earth here and a crumb there, and in flood time sweeping away the looser projections of its bank. For years the alder had known that its time was coming; no roots could hold out against it. In the drowsy middle of the day, on Friday, there had been no wind, no extra water down the river; but the alder's time had come. It slid a little, toppled a little, and then fell—fell right across the river, bridging it from side to side.

The people of the house were exceedingly annoyed at the damage done to their grass and flowers. They spent the rest of Friday ringing up the farmer from whose land the alder had fallen, but the farmer wasn't going to do anything about a fallen tree until after the weekend; and *they* certainly did not intend to, they said.

They did not know about Pat. After school on Friday, he found his hole in the fence and, beyond it, the new tree bridge to take him across to the far bank of the river.

Then, he had had no time to explore; now, he had.

"Come on!" he told Lucy, and she followed, trusting him as she always did. They forced a passage through the outer branches to the main trunk. The going was heavy and painful. Pat, because he was just ahead of Lucy, shielded her from the worst of the poking, whipping, barring branches; but still he heard from behind him little gasps of hurt or alarm. More complaint than that she would not make.

They got footholds and handholds on the main trunk, and now Pat began—still slowly and painfully—to work his way along it to the far bank. The last scramble was through the tree roots, upended at the base of the trunk, like a plate on its edge. From there he dropped onto the riverbank of that unknown, long-desired country.

And now he looked back for Lucy. She had not been able to keep up with him and was still struggling along the tree trunk, over the middle of the river. She really was too little for this kind of battling—too young; yet Pat knew she would never admit that, never consent to his leaving her behind.

As he watched her creeping along above the water, he was struck by the remembrance that Lucy could not swim. But she was not going to fall, so that did not matter. Here she was at the base of the trunk now, climbing through the tree roots, standing beside him at last. Her face, dirtied and grazed, smiled with delight. "I liked that," she said. She put her hand in his again.

They began to move along the riverbank, going upstream. "Upstream is towards the source of the river," said Pat. "We might find it. Downstream is towards the sea."

"But I'd like to go to the seaside," said Lucy, halting. "Let's go to the seaside."

"No, Lucy. You don't understand. We couldn't possibly. It's much too far." He pulled her again in the upstream direction.

A ginger-coloured, puppyish dog had been watching them from one of the gardens on the other side. They noticed him now. He stared and stared at them, then gave a bark. Before Pat could prevent her, Lucy had barked back—rather well and very provocatively.

"Hush!" said Pat; but he was too late, and Lucy barked again. The dog had cocked his head doubtfully at Lucy's first bark; at the second, he made up his mind. He began to bark shrilly and continuously and as if he would never stop. He pranced along his section of the bank, shrieking at them as they went.

"Now look what you've done!" Pat said crossly. "Somebody will hear and guess something's up."

Lucy began to cry.

"Oh, I didn't mean it," said Pat. "No one's come yet. Stop it, do, Lucy. Please."

She stopped, changing instantly from crying to the happiest smiling. Pat ground his teeth.

The dog continued barking, but soon he could keep level with them no longer, for a garden fence stopped him. He ran up and down the length of it, trying to get through, banging his body against it. He became demented as he saw Lucy and Pat going from him, curving away with the riverbank beyond all possible reach. They heard his barking long after they had lost sight of him.

And now the nettles began. At first only a few, but at the first sting Lucy made a fuss. Then the clumps grew larger and closer together. They might have tried skirting them altogether, by moving in an arc from the riverbank; but in that direction they would have been stopped by another stream, flowing parallel to their own, and not much narrower. They could see that very soon the nettles were filling all the space between the two streams.

Pat considered. He had foreseen the possibility of nettles that afternoon, and was wearing a long-sleeved sweater as well as jeans and socks and sandals. Lucy and Lucy's mother, of course, had foreseen nothing: Lucy was wearing a short-sleeved dress, and her legs were bare. Legs always suffered most among nettles, so Pat took off his sweater and made Lucy put it on like a pair of curiously constructed trousers, with her legs thrust through the sleeves. Then he found himself a stick and began beating a way for them both through the nettle banks.

Whack! and *whack!* left and right, he slashed the nettle stems close to the ground, so that they toppled on either side and before him. Then he trampled them right down, first to one side, then to the other. Then again *whack! whack!* and trample, trample. From behind him Lucy called, "I'd like to do that."

"Oh, I daresay!" he said scornfully.

"Aren't you coming back for me?" she asked next, for his beaten path had taken him almost out of sight. So he went back to her and took her pickaback for some way; then decided that didn't help much, and was too tiring anyway. He put her down, and she waited behind him while he whacked. She kept her sleeved legs close together and hugged her bare arms close round her, against the nettles.

The nettles were always there—*whack! whack!* and trample, trample—until suddenly they stopped. There was an overflow channel from the river, man-made of brick and stone and cement patchings; it was spanned by a rather unnecessary bridge with a willow weeping over it. Lucy settled at once on the bridge under the willow to serve tea with leaves for plates and cups, and scrapings of moss for sandwiches, fancy cakes, and jellies. She was very happy. Pat took off his sandals and socks and trod about in the thin film of water that slid from the upper river down the overflow channel into the lower stream. He climbed about on the stone stairs down which the overflow water ran, spattering and spraying, to its new, lower level. The wateriness of it all delighted him.

Then the barking began again. There, on the other side of the river, stood the gingery dog. By what violence or cunning he had got there, it was impossible to say. It was certain, however, that he would bark at them as long as he could see them. Some loose stones were lying in the overflow and Pat picked up several and threw them at the dog. Those that did not fall short, flew wide. The dog barked steadily. Lucy left her tea party and descended onto a slimy stone to see what was happening, and the sliminess of the stone betrayed her: she slipped and sat down in the inch of water that flowed to the lower stream, and began to cry. Pat was annoyed by her crying and because she had sat down wearing—and wetting—

his sweater, and above all because of the ceaseless barking on the other bank.

He hauled Lucy to her feet: "Come *on*!"

Beyond the overflow there were fewer nettles, so that they went faster; but the gingery dog still kept pace with them, barking. But Pat could see something ahead that the dog could not: a tributary that joined the main river on the dog's side and that would check him, perhaps, more effectively than any garden fence. They drew level with the tributary stream; they passed it; and now they were leaving the gingery dog behind, as well as the nettles.

They entered a plantation of willows, low lying and neglected. Saplings had been planted here long ago for the making of cricket bats; then something had gone wrong, or perhaps the trees had been forgotten. Cricket was still played and willow bats used for it; but these particular willows, full grown and aging, had never been felled for the purpose. So, in time, like the alder downstream, many of them had felled themselves. Ivy, which had made the plantation its own, had crept up the growing trees and shrouded the fallen ones with loose-hanging swathes of gloomy green.

Lucy was charmed with the place and would have liked to resume the tea party interrupted under the weeping willow. Here were tree stumps for tables, and—an improvement on the overflow—meadowsweet and figwort on the riverbank that could be picked for table decoration. But she would not be left behind if Pat were going on.

Pat saw his chance. "I won't leave you behind," he promised, "but you can play while I just have a look ahead at the way we must go. Then I'll be back for you." Lucy accepted that. He left her choosing a tea table.

So, for a very little while, the afternoon became as Pat had planned it: just for himself. He went on through the sad plantation and came to the end of it—a barbed wire fence beneath which it would not be too difficult to pass. Beyond lay more rough pasture. Far to the right he saw the occasional sun-flash of cars on a distant road. But he was interested only in the river. Looking, he caught his breath anxiously, for a punt was drifting downstream. The only occupant, however, was a man who had shipped his pole in order to drift and doze in the sun; his eyes were shut, his mouth open. He would not disturb Pat and Lucy, if they did not disturb *him*.

Shading his eyes against the sun, Pat looked beyond the punt, as far as he could see upstream. The river appeared very little narrower than at the fallen alder, so probably he was still far from its source. Still the riverbank tempted him. He could see it curving away, upstream and out of sight. Even then he could mark the course of the river by the willows that grew along it. In the distance he could see the top of a building that seemed to be standing on the river; perhaps a mill of some kind, or the remains of one; perhaps a house . . .

Anyway, he would soon see for himself.

He had actually stooped to the barbed wire fencing when he remembered Lucy. Recollecting her, he had also to admit to himself a sound coming from where he had left her, and that had been going on for some time: a dog's furious barking. He sighed and turned back.

Back through the sad plantation to the part of the riverbank where he had left Lucy. "Lucy!" he called; and then he saw the dog on the opposite bank. Its gingeriness was darkened by the water and mud it had gone through in order to arrive where it was. For a wonder, it had stopped barking by the time Pat saw it. It sat there staring at Pat.

"Lucy!" Pat called, and looked round for her. There on a tree stump were her leaf plates, with crumbs of bark and heads of flowers; but no Lucy.

His eyes searched among the trees of the plantation, and he called repeatedly, "Lucy! Lucy! Lucy!"

There was no answer. Even the dog on the opposite bank sat silent, cocking its head at Pat's calling, as if puzzled.

It was not like Lucy to wander from where he had left her. He looked round for any sign of her beside the tea table. He noticed where she had picked meadowsweet and figwort; stems were freshly broken. A wasp was on the figwort. Lucy was afraid of wasps, but perhaps the wasp had not been there when she had picked what she wanted. The figwort with the wasp on it leaned right over the water.

"Lucy!" Pat called again. He went on calling her name while he slowly swivelled round, scrutinizing each part of the willow plantation as he faced it. He came full circle, and was facing the river again.

The river flowed softly, slowly, but it was deep and dark. Every so often, perhaps at distances of many years, somebody drowned in it. Pat knew that.

He looked over the river to the dog and wondered how long he had been there, and why he had barked so furiously, and then stopped.

He looked at the bank where the figwort grew: it was crumbly, and now he noticed that some of it had been freshly broken away, slipping into the water.

He saw the flowing of the water, its depth and darkness. Speechless and motionless he stood there, staring.

The summer afternoon was still perfect, with sunshine, flowers blooming, birds singing, even to the cuckoo. . . .

Then suddenly: *the cuckoo*! He swung round, almost lost his balance on the edge of the riverbank, and, with a shout of "Lucy!" started off in quite the wrong direction. Then he saw a hand that lifted a curtain of ivy hanging over a fallen tree trunk. He plunged towards it and found her. She was hiding in a green ivy cave, laughing at him. He pulled her out, into the open, and began smacking her bare arms, so that she screamed with pain and astonishment and anger. The dog began barking again. Pat was shouting, "You stupid little girl—stupid— stupid—stupid!"

And then another voice was added to theirs, in a bellow. The punt Pat saw earlier had come downstream as far as the plantation, and the man who had been dozing was now on his feet and shouting, "Stop that row, for God's sake! And you ought to be ashamed of yourself—beating your sister like that! Stop it, or I'll come on land and stop you myself with a vengeance!"

The two children stared, still and silent at once. Then Pat gripped Lucy and began to pull her away from the riverbank and the man and the dog. They blundered through the plantation and reached the barbed wire. They crept under it, and Pat set off again, pulling Lucy after him, across the meadows to the right, towards the distant road.

"We're going home," he said shortly when Lucy, in tears, asked where they were going.

"But why aren't we going back by the riverbank and over the tree? I liked that."

"Because we're not. Because I say so."

When they reached the road, they turned in the direction of home. There was a good way to go, Pat knew, and Lucy was already grizzling steadily. She hated to walk when she had to walk. There was not much chance of anyone they knew stopping to give them a lift and, if anyone did, there would be a lot of questions to be answered.

They passed a bus stop and plodded on. Lucy was crying like a toothache. Pat heard a car coming and it passed them. Later, a lorry, and it passed them. Then there was a heavier sound behind them on the road, and Pat turned: "Lucy, quick! Back—run back!"

"Back?"

But Pat was already dragging her with him back to the bus stop, signalling as he ran. The bus drew up for them and they climbed in and sat down. Pat was trembling. Lucy, who had needed a handkerchief for some time now, passed from sobbing to sniffing.

The conductor was standing over them. "Well?" he said.

Pat started. "Two halves to Barley," he said.

The conductor held out his hand.

Pat felt through all the contents of his trouser pockets, but before he reached the bottoms he knew, he remembered: "I've no money."

The conductor reached up and twanged the bell of the bus and the driver slowed to a halt, although there was no bus stop. "I've a heart of gold," said the conductor, "but I've met this trick before on a Saturday afternoon."

Pat could feel the other passengers on the bus were listening intently. Their faces, all turned in his direction, were so many pale blurs to him; almost certainly he was going to cry.

The conductor said, "You've some hard luck story, no doubt, you and your little sister."

"She's not my sister."

A voice from somewhere in the bus—the voice of Mrs. Bovey, who lived down their road—said, "I know him. He's Pat Woods. I'll pay the fare. But what his mother would say . . ."

"You're a lucky boy, aren't you?" the conductor said.

Pat did not look at Mrs. Bovey; he did not thank her; he hated her.

The conductor took Mrs. Bovey's money and twanged the bell again, so that the bus moved on. He held out two tickets to Pat, but did not yet let him take them. "Latest fashion, I suppose?" he said. Pat did not know what he meant until he pointed, and then Pat realized that Lucy was still wearing his sweater as trousers.

"Take that off," Pat ordered Lucy. As she was slow, he began to drag the sweater off her.

The conductor interrupted to hand him the tickets. "You be gentle with your sister," he warned Pat; and from somewhere in the bus a passenger tutted.

"She's not my sister, I tell you."

"No," said Mrs. Bovey, "and what *her* mother will say I don't like to think."

"You'll grant you're in charge of her this afternoon?" said the conductor. "Speak up, boy."

In the silence, Lucy said, "You're making him cry. I hate you. Of course he looks after me. I'm always safe with him."

Pat had turned his head away from them—from all of them—as the tears ran down his cheeks.

Maurice's Room

Paula Fox

THE COLLECTION

Maurice's room measured six long steps in one direction and five in the other. The distance from the floor to the ceiling was three times higher than Maurice. There was one window through which Maurice could see several other windows as well as a piece of the sky. From the middle of the ceiling dangled a long string, the kind used to tie up packages of laundry. Attached to the end of the string was a dried octopus. It was the newest addition to Maurice's collection. When his mother or father walked into his room—which wasn't often—the octopus swung back and forth a little in the draft.

Maurice had used a ladder to climb up high enough to tack the string to the ceiling. The ladder was still leaning against the wall. Instead of returning it to Mr. Klenk, the janitor of his building, from whom he had borrowed it,

Maurice was using the steps for shelves. Even though Maurice's father, Mr. Henry, had put up a dozen shelves around the room for all of Maurice's things, there still weren't enough.

Maurice knew how to walk around his room without stepping on anything, and so did his friend Jacob. But no one else did.

As his mother and father often said to visitors, it was astonishing how much junk a person could find in one city block. His mother said Maurice kept their block clean because he brought up everything from the street to his room. His father said Maurice ought to get a salary from the Department of Sanitation because of all the work he was doing in cleaning up the city. At least once a month Mr. and Mrs. Henry talked about moving to the country. It would be better for Maurice, they said. But then they would decide to wait a little longer.

Some visitors said that collections like Maurice's showed that a child would become a great scientist. Many great scientists had collected junk when they were eight years old. Other visitors said Maurice would outgrow his collection and become interested in other things, such as money or armies. Some suggested to the Henrys that they ought to buy Maurice a dog, or send him to music school so that his time might be spent more usefully.

In his room Maurice had a bottle full of dead beetles, a powdery drift of white moths in a cup without a handle, a squirrel hide tacked to a board, a snakeskin on a wire hanger, a raccoon tail, a glass of shrimp eggs, a plate of mealy worms, a box of turtle food.

There were things with which to make other things, such as nails of different sizes, screws, wire, butterfly bolts, scraps of wood, sockets, filaments from electric light bulbs, cardboard from grocery boxes, two orange crates, a handsaw, and a hammer. On the top of a chest of drawers, Maurice kept stones and pebbles, dried tar balls, fragments of brick, pieces of colored bottle glass that had been worn smooth, and gray rocks that glistened with mica.

On his windowsill, there was a heap of dried moss next to a turtle bowl in which several salamanders lived half hidden by mud and wet grass. On the same sill, he kept some plants from the five-and-ten-cent store. They looked dead. Now and then a cactus would put out a new shoot.

In another bowl on a table covered with yellow oilcloth were four painted turtles that were getting quite soft in the shell, and in a corner, in a square fish bowl with a chicken-wire roof, lived a garter snake and a lizard. An old hamster in his cage slept or filled his pouches with dried carrots or ran on his wheel. The wheel, which needed an oiling, screeched all night, the time the hamster preferred for exercise. But the noise didn't keep Maurice awake, only his parents. In a pickle jar, a garden spider sat in a forked twig, her egg sack just below her. Maurice also had a bird. It was a robin, blind in one eye and unable to find food for itself.

On the floor were coffee cans with things in them; an eggbeater with a missing gear, a pile of dead starfish, cigar boxes, clockworks, hinges, and a very large grater with sharp dents on all four of its sides. The grater was orange with rust, and it stood in the middle of the room beneath the octopus. You would have to use a magnifying glass to see all the other things Maurice had found.

His bed had two blankets and a pillow without a pillowcase. Sometimes a small goose feather pricked its way through the ticking, and Maurice would put it away in an envelope. He had used two pillowcases for his collecting expeditions, and after that his mother wouldn't give him any more.

There was one tidy corner in Maurice's room. It was where he had pushed his Christmas toys. They were a month old now, and the dust covered them evenly. They were like furniture or bathroom fixtures. Maurice felt there wasn't much to be done with them.

"GET EVERYTHING OFF THE FLOOR"

It was the end of January, and Maurice had just come home from school. He put his books on his bed and went to see what the snake was doing. It was lying on its rock. The lizard was watching it. The robin was so still it looked stuffed. But it cocked its head when Maurice whistled at it. The hamster was hiding bits of carrot in the sawdust at the bottom of its cage. The salamanders had buried themselves in the mud. Maurice was arranging little piles of food for his animals when he heard his uncle's voice from down the hall.

"Lily," his uncle was saying to his mother, "you ought to dynamite that room!"

"There must be another way," his mother said.

"You'd better give it up," said his uncle. "Maurice will never clean it."

"If we lived in the country, it would be different," said his mother.

"Perhaps," said his uncle.

Maurice took two walnuts from his pocket and cracked them together. His mother came to the door.

"Get everything off the floor," she said in a low, even voice as though she were counting moving freight cars.

"Where will I put things?" asked Maurice.

"I don't care," she said. "But clear the floor! Or else I'll bring in the broom, the dustpan, and a very large box. And that will be that!"

The doorbell rang. It was Jacob.

"Jacob can help you," his mother said.

Jacob was seven, but he looked bigger than Maurice. It was because he was wearing so many clothes—scarves, mittens, sweaters, two hats, and several pairs of socks. He began to take off his outer clothing, laying each item in a pile at his feet. Meanwhile Maurice explained the predicament.

"What are we going to do?" asked Jacob.

99

Maurice looked at the chest of drawers. The pebbles and rocks had been moved to the floor, and the chest was now covered with oatmeal boxes. He looked at the table. He could barely see the yellow oilcloth because it was hidden by sections of a witch doctor's mask he and Jacob had begun to make the week before. The turtles had been moved next to the salamanders on the windowsill.

"There are five more floors in this room if you count the walls and ceiling," Maurice said to Jacob. Jacob looked smaller and thinner now that he was down to his shirt and pants.

"I see," said Jacob.

"We'll have to ask Mr. Klenk to help us," said Maurice.

Jacob began to sort out nails. Then he stopped. "But we won't be able to do that with everything! And how can we get it all done in just a day?"

"Mr. Klenk will know," said Maurice.

THE JANITOR

Mr. Klenk, the janitor, lived in the basement five floors down. The basement smelled like wet mops, damp cement, pipes, and old furniture stuffing. But it was clean. Mr. Klenk had told Maurice that he couldn't relax a second or he would be drowned by the rubbish that poured out of all the apartments. "Overwhelming!" Mr. Klenk often exclaimed.

"It's a race between me and the junk," he would say. "If I let it get an edge on me, I'll get shoved right out of the city." But Mr. Klenk didn't seem to feel the same way about Maurice's collection.

"Well, you're selective, my boy," he had said once, giving Maurice a caramel. "Besides, I suspect you've got something in mind for all that stuff of yours."

The two boys rang the janitor's bell. Mr. Klenk opened his door, blowing out a cloud of cigar smoke.

"I have to get everything off the floor," Maurice said. "Could you help us a little?"

"What do you have in mind?"

"There's plenty of space on the walls," said Maurice.

Mr. Klenk nodded and puffed on his cigar. "I know," he said. "But you didn't bring back my ladder, did you?"

"He forgot," said Jacob timidly. Mr. Klenk peered through the cigar smoke. Jacob backed away. The janitor in the building where Jacob lived sat in a big collapsed steamer trunk all day just waiting, Jacob was sure, for boys to wander by so he could pounce on them.

"Can you come now?" asked Maurice.

"Let's go," answered Mr. Klenk.

When they reached Maurice's room, Mr. Klenk stopped at the doorway.

"How am I supposed to get in there?" he asked.

Jacob cleared a path for him. Maurice took all the things off the ladder steps, and in a few minutes Mr. Klenk was at work.

First Maurice chose the starfish. He handed it to

101

Jacob, who held it up to Mr. Klenk on the ladder. Next came the rusty grater. In an hour everything was hanging either from the ceiling or from the walls. The animals paid no attention to the fact that they were suspended above the floor. The hamster went to sleep; his cage swung gently like a hammock in a light breeze.

By six o'clock, the floor boards appeared. It was a good floor, and Maurice and Jacob sat down on it.

"Now we have room for more things," said Maurice.

Maurice's mother and his uncle came to the door.

"Wow!" said Uncle.

Mrs. Henry looked pale. "I didn't have *that* in mind," she said.

"Well, Lily, they've cleared the floor," said the uncle. He looked at Maurice. "I have a surprise," he said. "I'm going to bring Patsy here to spend a week with you."

Then his uncle winked at Mrs. Henry. "You'll see," he said to her. "Patsy will take his mind off all of this." Maurice's mother looked doubtful.

"Who is Patsy?" asked Jacob.

"Who is Patsy!" repeated the uncle, as though astonished. "Tell him, Maurice."

"A dog," said Maurice. "A dumb fat dog," he added in a whisper to Jacob.

After Maurice's uncle and Mrs. Henry went back to the kitchen, Mr. Klenk picked up his ladder and started to leave. Then he seemed to remember something. He tapped Maurice on the shoulder.

"Would you like a stuffed bear?" he asked.

"I'd like a bear," Maurice said.

"A tenant left it when he moved out," said Mr. Klenk. "Send your man down for it in the near future." He nodded at Jacob.

"We could make a car for it," said Maurice after Mr. Klenk had left.

"There's a busted baby carriage in front of my building," said Jacob.

"Bring the wheels," said Maurice.

Jacob began to put on all his outdoor clothes.

"I never heard of a bear having a car," he said.

"Why not?" asked Maurice.

THE DOG

Maurice and Jacob were unable to begin building a car for the bear the next day because Patsy arrived early in the morning.

Patsy was a large soft dog with beady eyes. She was wearing a plaid wool coat. Maurice and she stared at each other for several minutes. She was nearly as tall as he was. Then she walked straight into Maurice's room. When she came out a minute later, she had an oatmeal box in her mouth.

"Give me that!" demanded Maurice. Patsy lowered herself slowly on her four legs until she was lying on the floor with the box in her teeth.

Maurice looked at his mother. She was smiling and nodding. He looked at his father, who was just about to leave for work.

"Nice dog," said his father.

"Give it back," whispered Maurice to Patsy. She stared at him. Then she turned her head suddenly, and Maurice snatched the oatmeal box and ran to his room with it. He closed the door and went back to the kitchen to finish his bacon and cocoa.

When he came out to put on his galoshes before going to school, Patsy was sitting in the living room. She was chewing an ear section of the witch doctor's mask. He ran to her and grabbed it. Patsy stood up and wagged her tail. Maurice could see she was just waiting for him to leave. He pretended to go to the front door, then suddenly turned and tiptoed back to his room. Patsy was already in it, sniffing up at the hamster.

"Please leave my room," said Maurice. Patsy looked at him over her back. He slipped his fingers beneath her collar and pulled. It was difficult to drag such a big dog. His mother came to the door. "Don't bully the dog," she said. "Good Patsy!"

"I don't want her in my room," said Maurice.

"She's so friendly," his mother said. Patsy wagged her tail and sat down on Maurice's foot.

"She was trying to eat the hamster," Maurice said.

"Oh!" exclaimed his mother. "You're exaggerating! She was only looking around. She probably misses your uncle."

Maurice looked at a round hole in his door near the knob where he and Jacob had dug out the lock and the latch months ago.

"Couldn't we put the lock back in?" he asked.

"Not now," said Mrs. Henry. "Now you go to school. You're going to be late!"

Right after his arithmetic class, Maurice asked the teacher for permission to go to the principal's office. The secretary said he could use the telephone for two minutes.

"Hello," said Maurice's mother.

"Is she in there?" asked Maurice.

"Who?" asked Mrs. Henry.

"Pull the octopus higher," said Maurice.

"Oh, Maurice," said Mrs. Henry, "as if I didn't have enough to do! Patsy doesn't want your octopus."

Maurice looked up at the clock.

"Can't you tie her to something?" Maurice asked.

"Stop fussing," said Mrs. Henry.

After school, Maurice ran all the way home. He was out of breath when he reached his front door.

Patsy was lying asleep in the living room. Maurice's things were all around her like a fortress. Her head was resting on the raccoon tail.

It took Maurice an hour to put everything back. Patsy watched him from the door.

"Thief!" he said to her. She wagged her tail.

The next day Maurice did not feel very well. His mother said he could stay home provided he kept to his bed. "None of this wandering around in bare feet," she said.

Maurice was happy to stay in his room. He watched Patsy as she paced back and forth outside his door. When she tried to sneak in, he shouted, "No, you don't!"

That afternoon he heard his mother speaking with his uncle on the telephone.

"Maurice and Patsy are inseparable," she said. "You were quite right. We must get him a dog of his own."

"A whole week," said Maurice to himself. He began to feel really sick. Suddenly Patsy made a dash for the chest of drawers. She put one paw on a drawer pull.

"Out!" shouted Maurice, standing up in the middle of his bed with the blankets flapping around him. Patsy ran from the room, but she sat down right in front of the door.

The next day Maurice felt poorly again. His mother took his temperature. He had no fever. His throat wasn't red. But his eyes looked strained. The strain came from staring through the dark at Patsy half the night. But the dog had fallen asleep before Maurice had, and so she had been unable to steal a single thing from Maurice's room.

"I think you should go to school," said Mrs. Henry.

"No!" said Maurice, kneeling on his bed.

"Mercy! You don't have to kneel," she said. "What *is* the matter?"

"I can't go to school," Maurice said.

Mrs. Henry called Mr. Henry.

"I think he is developing a school phobia," Maurice heard her say to his father as they stood in the hall outside his room.

At that moment, Patsy raced in, threw herself at the bed, snatched a blanket, and made off with it. Maurice jumped to the floor and ran after her. They both slammed into Maurice's father.

"If you don't stop playing with Patsy, I'll have to send her home!" said Mr. Henry.

After that, it was easy. Maurice played with Patsy every minute he could, and soon his uncle came to get her. He dressed Patsy in her plaid coat, clipped on her leash, put on his hat, and left.

"You see?" said Maurice's father.

Maurice nodded.

THE BEAR

One Saturday morning, a few weeks after Patsy had left, Maurice awoke at six o'clock. His window was blurred because it was raining so hard. The hamster stirred in its cage.

"You're up too early," Maurice said. The robin lifted one wing slowly and opened its good eye. Maurice went into the kitchen and made himself a grape-jelly sandwich. It felt good to be eating a sandwich and walking down the hall so early in the morning. No one else was awake. He gave a piece of bread crust to the robin and one to the hamster. Then he got dressed.

Soon there was a soft knock on the front door. It was Jacob, who always arrived early on Saturday mornings and who usually brought something with him. Today he was carrying a paper sack.

"Do you want a jelly sandwich?" asked Maurice. Jacob nodded. Then he showed Maurice what he had brought in the bag.

"What is it?" asked Maurice.

"I think it's for weighing things. I found it in a box on the street," Jacob said, holding up a large white scale. The paint was chipped, and when Maurice pressed his hand down on the platform, the needle on the dial jiggled.

"Your arm weighs six pounds," said Jacob.

Maurice's mother walked by. She was yawning. She glanced into the room. "Good morning, children," she said.

"My arm is very heavy," said Maurice.

"That's nice," said Maurice's mother, and yawned again and walked on.

"I forgot to tell you," Jacob said. "Mr. Klenk said to come and get the bear."

Maurice put the scale on his bed. Then both boys ran to the front door and down the five flights of stairs to Mr. Klenk's room in the basement. Mr. Klenk was blowing on the cup of coffee he was holding in one hand. He still carried a broom in the other.

"It seems I hardly have time for coffee," said Mr. Klenk. "I'll be glad to get rid of that bear."

He left them standing at the door, peering into his room. There was so much cigar smoke in the air, it was hard to see the furniture. In a minute Mr. Klenk was back, pushing the bear before him. The bear's feet were strapped into roller skates. It was as tall as Jacob.

"Here he is," said Mr. Klenk. "Think you can handle him?"

Jacob and Maurice stared. The bear was plump. Its fur was black. Its two front paws stuck out straight in front of it. The claws were of different lengths, and some of them pointed upward as though the bear had been pushing against a wall.

"Why is it wearing skates?" asked Maurice.

"It came that way," said Mr. Klenk.

"It looks tired," said Jacob.

"It had a long sea voyage, all the way from South America."

Maurice pulled and Jacob pushed and they got the bear up the stairs all the way to Maurice's front door, and inside. Because of the skates the bear moved easily on a level surface, but it had been a slippery business getting it up the stairs.

"I think we'd better wait a while before we show it to my mother and father," said Maurice. "They don't like surprises."

"Mine neither," Jacob said.

Maurice said, "Why don't you get your hat and coat and put them on the bear and maybe they'll think it's you if we push him down the hall fast."

Jacob went to get his outdoor clothes. They dressed the bear, pulling Jacob's hat almost all the way down its muzzle. Then, running, they propelled it down the hall. As they went by his parents' bedroom, Maurice's father poked his head around the door.

"Who's that?" asked Mr. Henry in a sleepy voice.

"Jacob!" said Maurice.

"Maurice!" said Jacob.

Mr. Henry went back to bed. "You shouldn't roller-skate in the house," he said.

At last they got the bear into a corner of Maurice's room. "The bear has a funny smell," said Jacob.

"You're right," said Maurice. "But we'll have to get used to it."

They took Jacob's clothes off the bear. Then they stood and looked at it. It was pleasant to have a big animal in the room with them, even if it was stuffed.

"Maurice," Mrs. Henry called. "Come and drink your apple juice."

"We'll have to disguise it. Then one day when they're feeling good I'll just tell them I have a bear," said Maurice in a whisper. Then he called out, "We'll be there in a minute."

"Couldn't we hide it under the bed for a while?" asked Jacob.

"No," said Maurice. "It won't fit because the Victrola's there. But wait a minute." Maurice opened his closet door and pulled out a heap of clothing. Pretty soon he found what he wanted. It was a penguin costume.

"It was for Halloween," said Maurice.

They started dressing the bear. They had to cut holes in the feet to fit the costume over the bear's roller skates. Then they zipped up the front and pushed the bear between the table and the window. Nothing was left showing of it except the big bumps where its paws were.

Then they went to the kitchen and had apple juice and doughnuts.

PATSY AGAIN

The next day, which was Sunday, Maurice's uncle was coming to visit. When Maurice heard that Patsy was coming with him, he went to his room and began to pile up things behind his door.

Maurice's father knocked, and Maurice opened the door a crack.

"Maurice," he said, "you'll have to clean out the hamster's cage. There's a very strong smell coming from your room."

"All right," said Maurice. "I'll do it right now."

He looked at the bear in its penguin costume.

"I wonder if I could spray you with perfume," he said.

Then he took a piece of rope and tied one end of it around the bear's neck and the other to his bedpost. If somebody came in, he decided, he would just roll the bear out the window and then pull it back into the room when the coast was clear.

A few minutes later, he heard his mother let his uncle in at the front door.

"Well, Lily, how are you?"

"Fine, and you?"

"Fine, and your husband?"

"Fine, and Patsy?"

"Fine."

"Fine," said Maurice to the hamster.

"And how is Maurice?" asked the uncle.

"Fine," said his mother.

"He'll be delighted to see Patsy."

"He surely will be delighted."

Maurice added his boots to the heap behind his door.

A large object suddenly hurtled down the hall and against Maurice's door. It was Patsy. The barricade gave way, and Patsy raced into the room, stomping and huffing and panting. The snake slid under its rock, the lizard froze, the hamster burrowed in its sawdust, and the bird closed its good eye.

Patsy stopped dead in her tracks. Maurice stood up slowly from where he had been crouching near his bed. Patsy's nose was in the air. She was sniffing. She slid one floppy paw forward, then another. Maurice sprang toward the bear, his arms outstretched.

"Don't lay a hand on that bear!" he cried.

It was too late. Patsy leaped. Over and down crashed the bear. All eight wheels of the roller skates spun in the air. Patsy sat on the bear and began to bay. Maurice could hear his mother, his father, and his uncle racing down the hall.

He ran to the window, flung it open, and deposited the turtles on the floor. He grabbed a blanket from his bed and threw it over Patsy, who fell into a tangled heap alongside the bear. In a flash, Maurice had the bear up on its skates and on the sill. He gave it a shove, and out it went through the window, the rope trailing behind it.

Mr. Klenk, who was sweeping the courtyard below and whistling softly to himself, heard the whir of spinning roller skates and looked up.

"Ye gods!" he cried. "A giant penguin!"

THE TRUMPET LESSON

"Today you are going to start your trumpet lessons," said Mrs. Henry. She held out a black case that reminded Maurice of a crocodile's head. Maurice put it on his bed and opened it. The trumpet glittered. He could see his face reflected in it.

He looked out of his window. A light rain was falling, a March rain that might be warm. It was exactly the kind of Saturday Maurice and Jacob liked to spend hunting for new things for the collection.

"You'll have to leave very soon," said Mrs. Henry as she started back to the kitchen to finish her cup of coffee. Maurice lifted the snake out of its cage. The snake wound itself around his wrist. It was a dull green color and quite small.

"The trouble with you is you don't have enough interests," he said to the snake. He put it back in its cage and pulled the chicken wire over the top. Then he put on his light jacket.

When he got to the front door, his mother said, "Just a minute. Haven't you forgotten something?" She was holding out the trumpet case. "And Maurice, really! It's raining! Put on your rubbers and your heavy jacket."

"Maurice, you must learn to be more responsible," said his father, who was standing at the other end of the hall eating a piece of whole wheat toast.

Maurice went back to his room, dug into his closet, and found one of his rubbers and one of Jacob's. He wished he had been born wearing one pair of shoes and one suit of clothes.

Jacob was waiting for him in front of the building.

"Do your lessons really start today?" he asked.

"Yes," said Maurice. As he had guessed, it was a warm spring rain.

"Will you have to go every Saturday morning?"

"For six weeks," said Maurice. "Then they'll see."

"See what?" asked Jacob.

"If I get new interests."

On their way to the music school where Maurice was to take his lesson, they passed a big junkyard. A sign hung over the wire fence that surrounded the yard: *Auto Parts*. A man wearing a hat was walking around the piles of bumpers and tires and car bodies. Now and then he would kick an old fender.

"Why don't you wait for me in there," Maurice suggested. "Maybe you can find something good." The man with the hat walked into a little house not much bigger than a telephone booth. There was a small window in it. Maurice could see the man fiddling with a radio.

"Maybe he'll chase me away," said Jacob, looking at the man.

"I'll stay for a minute," said Maurice.

They walked toward the rear of the lot. The man looked out of his window but didn't seem to see them. He was chewing on a toothpick and still twisting the radio dials. Just behind the little house, Maurice and Jacob could see the long arm of a crane.

"Look at that!" said Maurice, pointing to a pyramid of heaped-up car parts. Poking out of the pile were hubcaps, fenders, tires, fan belts, radiator caps, pipes, window frames, steering wheels on shafts, and at the very top, lying on a car hood, a pair of headlights that looked almost new.

"We could use those headlights," said Maurice.

Jacob looked back at the little house. "He won't give them to us," he said.

"Maybe he'd make a trade," said Maurice.

"What could we trade?" asked Jacob.

"We'll think of something," Maurice answered. "But first we have to see those headlights."

"How will we get them?" asked Jacob.

"Climb," said Maurice. "See all the places you can put your feet?"

"Me?" asked Jacob.

"I think you can do it better. I'm heavier. If I tried it, everything might crash down," Maurice said.

"Are you going to ask him first if we can?" asked Jacob.

"He's not even looking at us," said Maurice.

Jacob put his right foot on a tire rim, then grabbed hold of the fender above him and brought his left foot up to another tire. Slowly he climbed toward the top, using the tires as steps.

Suddenly there was a loud clanging of metal, then bangs, screeches, and a crash. When the dust cleared, Maurice saw Jacob almost at the top of the pyramid, stretched out on a silver-colored car hood, clutching its sides.

The man ran out of his little house. When he saw Jacob, he threw his hat on the ground.

"What's the meaning of this!" he shouted.

"We'd like to make a trade," said Maurice.

"Trade! At a time like this?" bellowed the man. "Get off my property!"

"Help!" said Jacob in a weak voice.

"How will we get him down?" asked Maurice.

The man picked up his hat and jammed it back on his head. "Can't he fly?" he growled; then he turned and walked to the crane. He jumped up to the seat and began to push the levers around furiously.

"Don't worry," Maurice called up to Jacob. "He's going to get you down."

Jacob didn't answer. He wasn't scared now, and he rather liked being so high above the ground.

There was a grinding of gears and a maniacal roar as the man maneuvered the crane into position.

"Clear away," shouted the man to Maurice. Maurice ran back toward the little house and watched as the claw at the end of the cables lowered its jaw, then clamped onto the hood where Jacob lay, gripped it, and lifted it down slowly like a plate. Several tires dislodged by the crane rolled along the ground.

"Well, get up," said Maurice to Jacob. Jacob was feeling sleepy. He shook himself a little and stood up.

"How was it?" asked Maurice.

"Okay," said Jacob.

The man jumped down from the crane, picked up a tire, and kicked it so hard it rolled all the way back to the pile. Then he started toward them.

Maurice and Jacob hurried to the gate. But Maurice stopped suddenly and darted into the little house, where he placed the trumpet on top of the radio.

"It's too late for my lesson anyhow," he said to Jacob as the man yelled after them, "I've got a friend on the police force!"

On the way home, Jacob said, "What will your mother and father say?"

"Plenty!" said Maurice.

A BIRTHDAY PRESENT

In a few weeks Mr. and Mrs. Henry stopped mentioning the trumpet. After that, whenever Maurice happened to hear them, they were talking about moving to the country. "We'll have to move anyway, at the rate Maurice is going," Mrs. Henry said once. "If he puts one more thing in his room, he won't have a place to stand."

But Mr. Henry wanted to wait.

On a morning late in April, Mrs. Henry brought Maurice a glass of fresh orange juice on a little tray. There was a sign leaning against the glass. It read: "Happy Birthday to Maurice." She couldn't get into the room, so Maurice got up from his bed and went to the door to get the tray.

Jacob came at noon and they had a birthday lunch. Maurice blew out all of his nine candles but he forgot to make a wish. Then Mr. and Mrs. Henry brought in a large box.

Maurice looked inside. It was a three-foot-long sailboat. The rigging was made of cord. The sails were of canvas, the winches really turned, and the hatches could be taken off and put back. It had two masts.

"It's a ketch," said Maurice's father, who was sitting on the floor next to him. "Look at those lines! Some boat!"

"Will it really sail?" asked Jacob.

"It will," said Mr. Henry.

"Can we take it to the lake right now?" asked Maurice.

"Yes," said Mr. Henry. "But be very, very careful with it."

Maurice's mother smiled. "It's nice to see you so interested in something," she said to Maurice.

The two boys carried the boat to the park. They dropped their jackets on the grass and sat down on the cement ledge that ran all around the lake. Then they rigged the sails.

A brisk wind was blowing. Maurice and Jacob slid the boat into the water. Instantly, it raced toward the center of the lake, its sails puffed out with wind. The boys ran around to the other side, but Jacob suddenly stopped. His hair was blowing almost straight up.

"Come on!" shouted Maurice.

"Look!" said Jacob, pointing at the water. Two or three feet out from the shore, something glistened as the breeze lifted the water into small waves.

"Bedsprings," said Maurice.

"How can we get them?" asked Jacob.

Maurice sat down on the ground and took off his shoes and socks, but Jacob waded in after Maurice with his shoes on. The springs were heavy, and weeds were growing through them.

They dragged them onto the grass. Maurice put on his shoes and socks and jumped on the springs.

"We can borrow wire cutters from Mr. Klenk and make coils to put on our shoes."

"We can hook it up so it stretches across the room," said Jacob.

"I can pull it across the door so Patsy doesn't get through," said Maurice.

They picked up the springs and started home. Jacob's wet shoes squeaked.

Then Maurice stopped. "We forgot something," he said.

They dropped the springs and ran back to the lake. On the opposite side was the boat, its stern halfway up the cement ledge, its sails flapping.

"What are you going to tell them?" asked Jacob as they lifted the boat out of the water. The stern was smashed and the mainmast tilted.

"I don't know yet," answered Maurice.

"Could we say there was a little storm?"

"No, we'll have to tell them what really happened—that the boat went out of control," said Maurice.

"Because we weren't watching," said Jacob.

They put the boat on top of the springs; then with Maurice holding the front of the springs and Jacob the back, they started home.

At first, Maurice's father didn't say anything. Mrs. Henry told Jacob to go home and change his wet socks and shoes; then she went to the kitchen. Maurice heard her rattling pots and pans.

"If I had known you wanted bedsprings instead of a beautiful three-foot sailing ketch, I would have gotten you bedsprings," said Mr. Henry at last.

Maurice said nothing.

"Go to your room and think about what happened," said Mr. Henry.

Maurice put the sailboat under his bed next to the Victrola so he wouldn't have to look at it. He put a blanket on the bedsprings and sat down on them. One of the coils had come loose and was bobbing up beside him. He rested his arm on it.

He heard his parents talking the rest of the afternoon. His mother brought him a supper tray while it was still daylight.

Then Mr. Henry came and stood in Maurice's doorway. Maurice was still sitting on the springs.

"I have something to tell you," he said. "We have decided to move to the country as soon as school is over."

"How will I see Jacob?" asked Maurice.

"Jacob can take the bus. It's not very far. You can have a dog."

"Not Patsy!" asked Maurice.

"No," answered his father. "But your uncle has a racing bike he is going to give you. It's a little old, but it still goes."

"I'm sorry about the boat," said Maurice.

"Your mother and I are sorry too," said Mr. Henry. He came over and sat down next to Maurice on the bedsprings.

"They're still a little damp," he said.

Maurice gave him a corner of the blanket to sit on. They didn't speak about the sailboat. In fact, it was never mentioned again.

AN EXPLOSION

The Henrys moved to the country the day after school ended. Mrs. Henry said Maurice could take his collection if he could find something to pack it in. Mr. Klenk gave him an old steamer trunk with broken hinges. Jacob brought a length of rope to tie around it. Maurice was able to get everything into the trunk except the bedsprings. He gave them to Jacob.

The movers' truck drew up in front of Maurice's building around noon. Mr. Klenk, Jacob, and Maurice stood outside and watched the movers load the furniture on.

"I don't see how they can get all those things into the truck," said Jacob.

"They fit them together like a jigsaw puzzle," said Mr. Klenk.

The last items the movers brought down were Maurice's animals and his trunk. They placed the cages on top of bureaus at the front of the truck. They left the trunk at the back, near the tailgate.

"Can I ride in the truck with my things?" Maurice asked his father.

"If it's all right with the movers," said Mr. Henry.

Mr. Klenk waved his cigar at Maurice. "Come back and visit me," he said. "I'll keep an eye out for interesting things for your collection."

Jacob didn't say goodbye. He was coming out to visit the next day. He waved as Maurice hiked himself up onto the truck.

All the way through town, Maurice could see his mother and father driving behind in the rusty jeep they had bought for the country. But soon he lost sight of it as the truck pulled ahead.

Maurice walked to the front, winding through the furniture and crates, the boxes and baskets, to check up on his animals. The hamster was running on his wheel, but the robin, the snake, the lizard, and the salamanders were all asleep.

They turned off on a blacktop, then onto a dirt road. After that, the ride got bumpier. There were no buildings, no gasoline stations, no signs—only green hills and trees and birds sitting on telephone wires. Here and there a crumbling stone wall followed the curve of a hill. The sun was very warm, and the canvas curtains on either side of the truck's tailgate flapped back and forth.

All at once, there was a tremendous crash. The furniture rattled, the cages danced on top of the bureaus, the robin chirped, and the pots banged against each other. They had driven over a big bump. Maurice's trunk teetered as they rounded a curve, then flew out, hit a rock, and seemed to explode into the air. Maurice saw his collection flying in all directions, then drop out of sight down the hill.

The truck stopped just as the jeep arrived. Maurice's father came running up to Maurice and lifted him down. Then everyone went to look over the hill. Maurice's things lay scattered everywhere among the rocks and tall grass. Maurice sat down on the road.

Mrs. Henry knelt beside him.

"Wow!" said Maurice. "Did you see that?"

Mrs. Henry stood up.

"The whole trunk blew up!" said Maurice. "It flew out in the air and exploded!"

"You can start a new collection," said Mr. Henry.

But Maurice didn't hear him. He was thinking that even the paper sacks of water he and Jacob had once dropped from the roof to the courtyard hadn't made such a terrific noise. He had never seen anything like it.

MAURICE'S BARN

Maurice's new room had one window and a slanted ceiling that was so low that Mr. and Mrs. Henry couldn't stand up straight beneath it.

When Maurice awoke the morning after the move, a branch was tapping against the windowpane and there were leaf-shaped shadows on the floor. Maurice wondered if he could step from the window to the big round branches of the tree that stood just outside. Just beyond the tree, Maurice could see a red barn. As he stared at it, a flock of birds flew from under the barn roof, circled in the sunlight, and flew back.

The room was empty except for Maurice's animals and his suitcase and the bed. The fields outside seemed empty too, except for the tall grass. The house was silent.

In the kitchen Maurice found a package of saltines and a glass of milk he had been too tired to finish the night before after all the unpacking.

Maurice's father walked in and sat down at the table. It was the same one that had been in Maurice's room in the city.

"Did you see the pump?" asked Mr. Henry.

"What's that?" asked Maurice.

"Sometimes there are storms, and the electricity goes off. Then you can use the hand pump to get water. It's just outside the door."

Maurice poked his finger into a little hole in the oilcloth.

"What do you think of the country?" asked Mr. Henry.

"It's okay," said Maurice.

"You are making a large hole in the oilcloth, Maurice. Why don't you take a look outside? Have you been to the barn?"

Maurice tried to balance four saltines against one another.

"Jacob will be here soon," said Mr. Henry. "You can take him to see the stream."

"What's in it?" asked Maurice.

"All right, Maurice," his father said, "you know what's in a stream!"

Maurice ate half a saltine. He wasn't very hungry.

"You'll get used to it here," said Mr. Henry. "It's new now. But you'll find lots of things to interest you."

At the word *things,* Maurice looked up at his father.

"There's nothing but grass," he said.

"Take a look in the barn," said Mr. Henry.

On his way out, Maurice tried the pump. He had to use both hands. Nothing happened for a moment; then a stream of cold bluish water gushed out on his sneakers. He squashed his way through the tall grass and the brambles to the barn.

The biggest door was padlocked, but next to it was a small door, which hung half open from one hinge. He slipped inside.

He heard a great rustling of wings. For a moment he stood still, waiting for his eyes to get used to the dark. Then he looked straight up. The roof of the barn seemed miles above him. Small birds swooped through the rafters from which hung spider webs as big as trapeze nets. As soon as Maurice began to walk, an interesting musty smell arose from the floor. On his right were wooden stalls and on his left was an old hay wagon. One of its big wheels lay on the floor, half covered with hay. There were ladders of all sizes leaning up against the walls, and from the posts that supported the overhead rafters hung an extraordinary assortment of objects.

"Fish nets," said Maurice aloud. "A hoe, a rake, a bucket, another bucket, a bamboo pole with a line and three fish hooks, a dog collar, mousetraps, a leather jacket, a pitchfork, a lantern." There were many other things made out of leather or wood or metal, but he didn't know what they were.

A big shaft of sunlight fell across the floor. Maurice turned and saw his father standing in the doorway. Bits of hay and dust floated around him.

"Your mother has gone to get Jacob at the bus stop," he said.

Maurice noticed several lengths of chain and a tire tube hanging from a nail near the door.

"Do you like the barn?" asked Mr. Henry.

"Yes," said Maurice.

"That's where they used to keep the hay," said Mr. Henry, pointing to a platform above the wagon. "But I don't think we're going to have cows or horses." Just then Jacob came to the door. He was carrying a paper bag.

"Come in and see my barn," said Maurice.

Jacob stepped inside.

"What's in the bag?" asked Maurice.

"Jelly doughnuts and a wrench Mr. Klenk gave me to give to you."

Maurice cleared the hay off the rim of the wagon wheel, and they sat down to eat their doughnuts.

"Your mother said there was a stream we could fish in," said Jacob.

"Not yet," said Maurice. "We have to fix up this barn. We have to find out what's in it. We can repair things. Like this wheel. We'll put it back on the wagon. Then, when we get too hot, we can go to the stream."

"What do we do first?" asked Jacob.

"First we have to find out the name of everything," said Maurice.

"Why?" asked Jacob.

"Because that's how you begin," answered Maurice. "Okay?"

"Okay," said Jacob.

THE PRINCE
AND THE GOOSE GIRL

Elinor Mordaunt

Once there was a great prince who was so great a fighter that no one dared to deny him anything that he asked, and people would give up their houses and lands, their children, and even their own freedom rather than offend him. Everything the people had was his at the asking, they feared him so, and would all tremble and shake when he came thundering past on his war horse, whose hoofs struck great pieces of their fields from the earth as he passed, and whose breath was fire. And they feared his sword, which was so sharp that it wounded the wind as it cut through it, and his battle-ax that could cut the world in half—or so they said—and his frown that was like a cloud, and his voice that was like thunder—or so they said.

Only Erith, the goose girl, feared him not at all.

"He is only a man," she would say. "What you tell of his sword and his battle-ax and his great frown is all a child's tale. He is just a man. He eats and sleeps like other men; if you wounded him, he would bleed. Someday he will love a woman and be her slave for a while just as any other man is. I wouldn't give that for the great bully!" she added, and snapped her little fingers.

"Hee, hee, Erith, that's all very well," the folk would say. "Wait till you meet him thundering over the common. You will fly as quick as any of your geese, we wager."

"I wouldn't move. It's a man's place to make room for a lady, not a lady's place to make room for a man. I wouldn't move, I tell you." And Erith stamped her little foot. It did not seem to impress the village people much, perhaps because it was bare and made no noise on the soft, dusty road, and one needs to make plenty of noise in this world if one is to be noticed.

"A lady! A lady!" they shrieked. "A lord to make place for a lady! Listen to her. My Lady Goosey Gander! A fine lady indeed, with bare feet and no hat."

"There's lots that have shoes that are not ladies," said Erith. "Shoes won't make one, nor bare feet mar one. I'm a better lady than any of you, though, for I'd not run away for anyone, even that ugly old prince. Bah! He's not noble or good or brave; he's just ugly—an ugly great bully!"

"Wait a bit, Lady Goosey Gander, wait a bit. If ever you see him, you will forget all your fine tales. Why, he's as tall as the church."

"And as strong as the sea."

"Why, his hands are like oak trees."

"And he cares no more than death who he attacks."

"Neither do I care," said Erith, setting back her shoulders and tossing her chin. "All men are babies, anyhow!"

The village gasped. That she should dare! She, a chit of a goose girl, to talk of the terror of the whole countryside like that. "All men are babies!" Well, well!

"It's a good thing that you are only what you are, my girl," growled the blacksmith. "For if you were of any account and the prince heard what you said, I would not give a farthing for your life."

"Hee, hee, Lady Goosey Gander," hooted the children from that day as they passed her on the way to school, tending her geese up on the common; but she only laughed at them, for she was really and truly brave, you know, and really truly brave people do not trouble much about trifles.

One day one of the prince's men heard the children and asked Erith what they meant.

"They call me Lady Goosey Gander because I said I was as good a lady as the prince is a gentleman, and better, for I know enough to be civil and kind," answered Erith, quite unconcerned, busy peeling a willow wand with her little bone-handled knife. She wove these willow wands into baskets while she watched her geese, and sold them in the neighboring market town, for she was poor and had her old mother to keep. She did not stop her work as she spoke; it was more important to her than all the gentlemen or all the princes in the world. She wanted a bag of meal, and she wanted shoes before the winter began. That was her business; other people might attend to their own.

The gentleman was amused. He told his fellows at supper that night and there was much laughter over the goose girl's words. A page waiting at table told his fellows. And then the prince's own man told him as he helped him off with his armor that night.

The prince laughed a great, big, bellowing laugh, but the red swayed up into his face angrily all the same.

"Where does this chit live?" he demanded.

The manservant shrugged his shoulders. "No one knows where she lives; she is of so little importance she might well live nowhere. But she feeds her geese each day on the common above the cliffs to the east, between here and the sea. A barefooted, common little thing."

"There's one thing uncommon enough about her. She dares to say what she thinks about me, and that's more than any of you do. I hear that she is very ugly, though."

"Most terribly ugly, Your Highness," answered the man.

"And old," said the prince.

"Very old, Your Highness. Quite, quite old."

"And deaf, too."

"As deaf as a post, Your Highness. It's evident she has never heard what all your subjects say about you," agreed

the man, for he always did agree—he was too frightened
to do anything else.

"It is too evident she *has* heard," said the prince
grimly. "And she is not deaf."

"Oh, no, Your Highness."

"And she is young."

"Indeed the merest child, Your Highness."

"And beautiful."

"As beautiful as the day, Your Highness."

"Only a country girl, of course, quite uneducated."

"Quite uneducated, Your Highness, and—"

What else he was going to say remained unsaid, for he
was stooping over the prince's foot unbuckling his spurs
while he spoke, and the prince lifted his foot—quite
easily as it seemed—and with it lifted the man, quite
easily, but with such force that he bumped against the
ceiling, "plump!" and then came to the floor, "bump!"

There were several other men in the room. However,
they did not run to pick him up—they were too
frightened of their master. But the prince just put out the
toe of his other foot and touched him, and he rolled over
and over like a ball and down the stairs, limpitty,
limpitty, limp.

Then another came forward to undo the other spur,
and he was treated the same.

"Take them both out and bury them!" shouted the
prince. "And if they're not dead, bury them all the same!"
Then he got up and flung around his chamber. He
touched no one, but they all fled like hares.

After that he sat down in his great chair, bellowing for wine, and forbade any to go to bed or to sleep, while he sat there himself all night, railing at his men for cowards and fools, and drinking good red wine.

Next morning, directly it was light, the prince ordered his horse, Sable, to be brought around, mounted it, and rode like the wind to the common by the sea.

"That chit of a goose girl is as good as dead," remarked his manservant as best he could for a broken jaw; indeed, you never saw anything so broken; all his legs and arms seemed nothing but splints and bandages. However, it was a common enough sight in the court of that prince, and no one took much notice.

The prince thundered along on his great black horse and presently came to the common. In the middle of it, he saw a flock of white geese and a patch of faded blue, which was the smock of the goose girl, who was sitting on a bundle of willow rods, busy with her basket making.

The prince did not draw rein. He thundered straight on. He scattered the geese in every direction. He would have galloped right over the girl if his horse had not swerved just as its hoofs were upon her. Then he drew rein.

The girl's hands did not stop from her work, but her great blue eyes were straight upon the prince's fierce black ones.

"The beast is less of a beast than the master," she said, for she knew it was the horse that had refused to tread upon her.

The prince pulled his reins, rode back a little, then spurred forward at Erith; but again the horse swerved and, being held with too tight a hand to turn, reared back.

The girl was right under his great pawing black hoofs. But she laughed.

The horse dropped to earth so close that his chest was against hers, his head held high to escape striking her. The foam dropped from his bit; his eye seemed all fire.

The girl's face looked up like a flower from among the thick blackness of his flowing mane. And she laughed again.

This was more than the prince could stand. He stooped from his saddle. He put his great hand into the leather belt of Erith's smock and swung her up in front of him. There he held her with one hand in its iron glove, shook Sable's rein, and put his spurs to his side.

"I have a mind to ride over the cliff with you," said the prince.

"Ride over," laughed Erith. And she took the willow rod that was still in her hand and smote the horse's neck with it. "Over the cliff, brave horse, and a good riddance of a bad man it will be," said she.

But the horse swerved at the edge of the cliff. And the prince let him swerve. Then they turned and they raced like the wind, far, far.

"Are you afraid?" said the prince.

"Afraid!" laughed the girl. She leaned forward along the neck of the horse, caught one little hand around its ear and cried, "Stop!"

Sable stopped so suddenly that his black mane and long black tail flew out like a cloud in front of him.

The prince swore a great oath and smote him, but he did not move.

Then Erith, not willing to see him hurt, whispered, "Go!" And he went—like the wind.

Far, far and fast he went. The prince was brooding too savagely to heed where they were being carried, so that when at length they came to a swamp, the horse, with one of his mighty strides, was borne far into it and sank to his girths before his rider knew what was happening.

You may picture it. The man and the maid and the horse nearly up to their necks in black mud.

Erith was small and light as a bird. She sprang from the arms which were loosed to pull the reins; she caught at a tuft of grass here, at a shrub there, and in a moment was on dry ground, though black to the knees with mire.

But the prince was a tall, great man. He was all in his armor, very heavy, and he could not move except downward; but he flung himself from his horse.

"That's not so bad of him," thought Erith. "He cares to save it, for he himself would have a double chance on its back."

The fierce black eyes of the man and the laughing blue eyes of the goose girl met across the strip of swamp. His were as hard as steel, for he did not mean to beg his life from any such chit.

Erith moved away a little. "She is going to leave me," he thought, and grieved, for he did not wish to die.

The girl had disappeared among a group of trees, but in a moment she came back, dragging after her a large, thick bough. Then she picked her way cautiously, as near as possible to the edge of the swamp. A little sturdy tree was growing there. Erith undid her leather belt, pressed her back firmly against the tree, and strapped the belt around both it and herself. Then she stretched forward with the bough in both hands.

"Pull," she cried. And the prince pulled.

The little tree creaked and strained. The goose girl's face grew crimson. It seemed as if her arms must be pulled from her body; but she held on, and at last the prince crawled out.

Erith had only been muddied a little above her smock, but the prince was mud up to his armpits, and his face, too, was smeared where he had pushed his helmet back from his forehead with muddy hands. He said no word of thanks to the girl, for he felt that he looked a poor thing, and it made him angry.

"I would I had left you there," said the goose girl. "A thankless boor! You were not worth saving."

The prince said no word, but began to pull out his horse. Even then the maid had to help him, for it was very heavy and deeply sunk.

Once the horse was free, the maid moved over to a pool which lay at the edge of the swamp and began to bathe her feet and legs and wash the mud from the hem of her smock.

The prince got on his horse, with a great deal of clatter and grumbling, but she did not turn. They were many, many miles from home, the country was strange and wild, but there she sat, quite untroubled, paddling her feet in the water.

The prince put his spurs to his horse and galloped away. But the beast would not go freely, spur it as he would. And soon he gave in, let it turn, and so back to the goose girl.

She had dried her feet on the grass by now and was standing plaiting her long hair, eyeing herself in the pool and singing softly.

The prince drew rein close to her and stuck out one foot. "You may come up," he said.

"An' may it please you," corrected the goose girl very quickly, with her blue eyes full upon him.

"May it please you," repeated the prince with a wry smile at himself; and the maid put her foot on his and jumped lightly to the saddle before him.

Sable needed no spur then, but sprang into a light gallop.

"All this is mine," said the prince boastfully, waving his arm as they went.

"I would it belonged to a better man," answered the goose girl. "And sit quietly or I will have no comfort riding with you."

"And you belong to me also," said the prince savagely.

"Not I. I belong to myself, and that is more than you do."

"What do you mean by that?"

"No man belongs to himself who is the slave to evil temper and pride," answered Erith gravely and gently.

After a long ride they came to the common again. On the edge of it was a tiny cottage.

"Stop here," said the goose girl, "and I will get down."

But the prince clapped his spurs to his horse's side and they were off like the wind. Moreover, he held the goose girl's hands so tightly that she could not touch Sable's ear or lean forward and speak to him. And so they galloped on till they clattered over the drawbridge into the courtyard of the castle.

A curious couple they looked. The prince all caked with mud, the goose girl with her wet smock clinging around her bare ankles and her long yellow hair loose, hanging below her knees.

The prince did not get off his horse, but sat like a statue while all the lords and ladies, the captains and the men-at-arms, the pages and the servingmen—even down to the scullery boy—thronged on the terrace and steps and at every window to look.

There was a long silence. Then one lady, who thought she was pretty enough to do as she liked, tittered loudly.

"The Lady Goosey Gander," she said. "The Lady Goosey Gander."

The prince's brow grew like a thundercloud. He flung his reins to one of the waiting grooms and alighted, then gave his hand to Erith, who leaped down as lightly as a bird. Still holding her hand, he turned to his people.

"You are always wishing me to choose a wife," he thundered. "Well, I have chosen one, and here she is. You can call the parson to bring his book and get the wedding feast ready, for I will be married in an hour's time."

With that he pulled off his helmet and flung around to kiss the goose girl, but—

"Shame on you," she cried, "to think to marry a maid before you've asked her! You can marry the cat, for all I care." And with that she caught him a great blow across the face and flung free.

Such a slap, such an echoing, sounding slap. The people of the court did not wait to see what would happen, for they knew what the prince was like in one of his rages all too well, and fled into the palace like rabbits to their burrows—not even a face at the window was left. Only the goose girl did not run, but stood and laughed at the prince's reddened face.

He caught at her wrist, yet not roughly. "You *will* marry me!"

"Perhaps someday when you learn to speak civilly," she replied. And, feeling her wrist free, she marched off over the drawbridge and over the meadow across the common and so home. She had her own business to attend to.

Some of the prince's people came creeping back. "Shall we go after her, Your Highness?" they asked, thinking to get into his favor again; but he drove them from him with the flat of his great sword and with oaths and shouting, then flung off to his own chamber and sat there drinking red wine till the night was near over; and none of his court as much as dared to go to bed till he slept.

Next morning he was off again at dawn on his black horse across the common. There sat Erith among her geese, weaving baskets. The very horse neighed with joy at the sight of her sitting there in the sunshine, but the prince only scowled.

"Will you marry me?" said he.

"No," said she, "and that's flat—not till you learn manners, at least."

Then he got off his horse and took out his sword and killed all her geese.

"You will have to marry me now or starve, for you have lost all your means of getting a living."

But the girl only laughed and took the dead geese and began plucking them, moving over to the side that the wind blew toward the prince, so that the feathers flew and stuck all over his armor in every chain and crevice and crack; and threw such handfuls of down in his face that when he went to seize her he was powerless.

Next day Erith, having trussed the plucked geese, took them to the market and sold them for a gold piece.

As she came home singing, she met an army of men bearing osier rods. "What have the osiers done that they should all be cut in one day?" she asked.

"The prince sent us to cut them, Lady Goosey Gander," they answered, jeering. "There is not one left at the brook's edge now, and your basket making is spoiled."

141

But the goose girl only laughed and turned back to the town and bought wool with her gold piece.

Next day as she sat before the fire in her cottage spinning the wool into yarn to sell at the market, the prince came striding in at the little door, bent half double, for it was so low and he so tall with his helmet on his head.

"It is only old women who remain with covered heads in the house," said the goose girl. "Good morning, old dame."

The prince took off his helmet. Somehow her ways pleased him, for he was sick of soft speaking.

"Will you marry me?" said he.

"When you kneel to ask me," said she. "Not before."

Then in a rage he took all her yarn, flung it into the fire, and was out of the house and away, thundering on his great black horse. But the goose girl only laughed.

Then she took a pair of scissors and cut off her long hair, yellow as honey in the comb, and fine as silk. This she spun and wove into a scarf, the rarest scarf ever seen.

On the third day, having finished her work, she was up at dawn and walked off to the court of a king, many miles distant. There she sought the queen and sold her the scarf for twenty pieces of gold.

"But why did you cut off your beautiful hair?" asked the queen.

"It was just forever in the way," replied the goose girl. She told no tales. To begin with, she did not like them, and to end with she *did* like the prince—perhaps because he was as fearless and obstinate as she herself.

Passing through the town, she bought a bag of meal and porridge. "The bag will do to cover my bare poll when it rains," she said to the merchant, and laughed. The gold jangled in the pocket of her petticoat and she felt as gay as a cricket.

On her way back she met the prince, who pulled up his horse and scowled at her, that she might not see the love in his eyes. Her head was all over little golden curls that shone in the sunlight.

"What have you done with your hair?" he asked.

"What have you done with the osiers and the feathers?" she asked in return, and laughed.

"Are you starving yet?"

"Far from it. I am richer than I ever was," and she shook her pocket till all the gold danced, for she feared nothing. But it was a foolish thing to do, for in a moment he had whipped out his sword and cut the pocket clean from the petticoat.

"Now will you marry me?" he asked, and held the pocket high and rattled the gold.

"Not I," she said, "if you are so poor that you'd have to live on your wife's earnings." And went her way singing.

The prince was ashamed of himself. He had never felt like it before, and it was very uncomfortable; it made him feel all tired and hot. It was all the goose girl's fault, of course, and he was very angry. But still he wished he had not stolen her money, and the thought of her little shorn head with its dancing curls made him feel for the first time in his life that he had a heart, and that it hurt.

So wrapped in his shame was the prince and sitting on his horse so loosely, and so heedless of everything that some robbers coming along the road took courage at the sight of him, for he did not look at all terrible as he usually did, and the gold rattled pleasantly. They had passed him many times before and kept their distance; but now they were emboldened to fall upon him, and so sudden was the attack that he was cast from his horse, the gold was gone, and he bound and gagged before he had thought to resist. Such a poor thing can shame make of any one of us.

Before they had finished, Sable had galloped away. "Shall we ride after him?" asked one of the robbers.

"No, no," answered the others. "He is too well known and we should surely be caught." So they mounted their horses and went off, leaving the prince bound and more ashamed of himself than ever. But Sable had galloped straight to the goose girl's cottage and struck at the door with his hoof.

When Erith opened the door, she was amazed to see the horse without his master. He muzzled his soft nose over her neck and hand, then trotted a little distance, then neighed as if to call her and returned. This he did several times.

"There must be something wrong," thought the girl; and she put her foot in the stirrup and leaped to the saddle. "Go like the wind," she whispered, leaning along his neck with one little hand around his ear. And like the wind he went.

Now, the robbers had not much rope to spare, so they had bound the prince kneeling with his arms pulled back and tied to his ankles behind him. And mighty uncomfortable it was. Besides, they had stuck one of their own foul handkerchiefs in his mouth and tied another across and around it. "Anyone who finds me will make a fine mock of me," thought the prince. And he seemed to burn with rage and shame.

But when the goose girl drew up beside him, *she* did not laugh, rather gave a little moan of pity, for the robbers had struck him wantonly over the head and the blood which he could not reach to stanch ran down over his face and eyes.

In a moment she was to the ground, had whipped out the little knife which she still carried in her belt, and cut the bandage and drew the gag from his mouth. She was turning to the ropes around the wrists and ankles then, when—"Stop!" said the prince.

Then, "Will you marry me, Erith?"

"It's a queer time to be asking that," replied the goose girl.

"You charged me to ask on my knees," answered the prince dryly, "and I am here. Will you marry me now?"

"An' it please you," corrected she, with calm blue eyes.

"An' it please you, dear heart," said he, almost meekly. "And we will not be living on your money, for it is all gone."

"Well, I don't mind if I do," answered the goose girl, and cut the ropes.

So they were trothed and kissed one another. And the prince put her on the front of his own horse and rode with her to the court, where he told the queen all that had happened and charged her, by her friendship, to get all manner of beautiful raiment and jewels ready and command a great feast that he might marry the goose girl one week from that day, she consenting.

It was the sunniest day ever known in all the world, and the gayest wedding and the fairest bride. And the feasting and dancing lasted for seven days, and there was none in the whole country who went hungry or without a share of the pleasures.

On the seventh day the prince took his bride back to his own kingdom. They would have no coach, but rode Sable over the hills and pastures and across the common where the geese had once fed, and over the drawbridge and home.

The new princess had little golden slippers on her feet now, and a robe of rose silk all embroidered with pearls, and a cloak of ermine. But her head was bare, with no crown save that of short golden curls.

THE BERMUDA TRIANGLE

Tim Wynne-Jones

Jim wrapped himself around the top of the tree like a flag around a pole. The September sky swayed in a slow circle above him, the tree in a slow circle under him. He got his breath, pushed his nerves down hard into the steel trap of his stomach, closed the lid on his fear. Then he waited a moment, breathing deeply, pumping himself up.

There was a wind up here. And a view. Locking his legs tightly around the tree trunk, Jim dared to let go with one hand. He was a sailor riding the crow's nest of a schooner. And there—the road past the farm—that was the sea. There was a good chop on it, for the pavement was cracked and heaving. It was a forgotten sea in a forgotten corner of the county.

Billy Bones was out there on that choppy sea in his '55 De Soto sedan, a frigate of steel and chrome. It plied the broken road in great springy leaps, bellying out between the buckles, the chassis scraping the road top. Billy headed up toward the highway. Then he drove back down a few moments later, heading toward his farm.

Jim started his tree swaying in the direction he wanted it to go. He held on with one hand, riding the tree now, leaning, leaning. It was maybe three meters to the next tree—another cedar, a twin in size to his mount. His dad would have said it was three yards. Either way, it would be his biggest leap so far.

Concentrate, Jim told himself. But then Billy Bones drove by again, up to the highway and back down. What was he up to? Was he picking up his mail at the lockbox one letter at a time? Was this what he did with his time? Was he as touched in the head as people said?

Jim turned his attention back to the task at hand. He gulped in fistfuls of air, swinging out and out, leaning, untangling his limbs from the tree until there wasn't much holding him. Then he was . . . leaping . . . falling . . . grabbing . . . holding on for dear life.

He pressed his body into the green embrace of the cedar, which swayed and dipped with the weight of him so near its crown. The fir tree poked him in the face, the gut, scraping his skin, cutting his hands.

But it was okay; he'd made it. Tightly he held on. He glanced behind him. The other tree still swayed with the memory of his weight in its branches.

It had happened again. Just as he leaped—just when there was nothing left to hold on to—he had made that sound. It started in his throat, and then it was outside him. A voice. *His* voice. He had a voice again.

He tried to speak, just say his own name. Nothing. It was gone. He could scream; why couldn't he talk?

Beyond the trees Billy Bones sailed his navy blue and cream yellow trawler up to the highway and back. Up and back, as if he were on patrol. Then, as Jim got his breath back, Billy coasted to a stop just near Jim's driveway. He climbed out of his car and looked up toward Jim, swaying against the slowly circling September sky.

Billy Bones scratched his head, looked out at the road. Looked as if maybe he were lost.

Jim slithered down through the branches, lithe as a squirrel—a flying squirrel—and landed with a thump on the grass. Billy was coming toward him up the drive. Jim watched him carefully, his fists clenched. He was ready to intercept the old guy, turn him around, send him home if he was going to tell on him.

"I seen your boy, Mrs. Hawkins, flying from tree to tree. Thought you'd want to know."

Who'd believe him anyway? The old man was touched in the head.

Billy came right up to Jim. He pointed to the car. "Runned outa gasoline," he said. "Got any gasoline on you, have you?"

Jim shook his head.

Billy looked toward the barn. Jim followed his gaze. For a minute he imagined his father coming out of the barn, coming to see what was up. But he didn't have a father anymore. Maybe Billy didn't know that. It was hard to guess what Billy might know.

Billy stared back out at his car. His shoulders fell. "You seen the box they got out there?" he said, pointing vaguely toward the road. "They got one of those box things out there on the road, *our* road. You seen it?"

Jim shook his head.

"Sure," said Billy. "One of those jobs from the Dee-partment of Highway Robbery. Got a long snake of a cord running out from it across the road. No doubting what that's for . . ."

He was agitated. His limbs jerked. Jim just held his ground. Waiting.

"That's right," said Billy, as if Jim had spoken. "A counter, see. Every time a car crosses that rubber cord, the box thing totes it up. That way they can tell how much this road is traveled upon."

Getting nothing, no reaction, from Jim, Billy looked out at the De Soto, scratched his chin, wiped his nose on the sleeve of his grimy jacket. Jim looked out at the road, too. Relaxed a bit. Billy hadn't come to tell on him.

Billy laughed. It was kind of like a series of hiccups. He didn't sound as if he'd had much practice laughing.

"I'll show 'em!" he said lustily, shaking his fist at the road. "I'll show that Dee-partment of Highway Robbery just how much traffic goes up and down our road. Do you know how many cars drove this road today?"

Jim shifted his weight, said nothing.

"Well, I'll tell you: thirty-six." Billy's old skin glowed with satisfaction, made him look as if there were rust around his eyes, his scabby lips.

Jim hadn't seen any cars go by today. Not anyone but Billy.

Billy laughed. "The traffic was all *me*."

He must have thought Jim had given him a look, because he cussed the boy suddenly. "You'll laugh out the other side of your face when they put down a spanking new asphalt pavement, boy. See what I'm getting at?"

Jim waited. This was what you did. Eventually people got the message that you couldn't talk to them and backed off. People who weren't touched in the head, that is.

The glow seeped away from Billy Bones's face. Now his skin looked like weathered barn board. But he stuck out his chin. "This week a thousand damned cars'll drive up our side road, Jim Hawkins. You see it? See the beauty of it? I'm sending a message. I'm getting us a road. A *real* road."

Then Billy's face cracked open to reveal a mouthful of teeth so crooked no dee-partment could have set them straight. He tapped the side of his head to show where he kept the machinery that had come up with this brainy idea. "Crazy like a fox," he said.

Jim stood as still as a tree. Waiting. Watching.

"Oh, I've heard all about you, Jim Hawkins. You ain't so dumb as you let on, are you, boy?" Billy turned and looked with confident expectation around the yard. There was no one. His expression crumpled. He looked back at Jim. "I'm sorry 'bout your dad," he said.

◆ ◆ ◆

They were neighbors, but until that September day Jim had never met Billy or even seen him up close. He was to see him three times that fall, three startling times, then never again.

The second time was on a dark late afternoon in October with the sun, too early, making its excuses on the horizon. Jim was out with a stick in the cornfield defeating an army of stubble that rose in sorry ranks around him. There was a dog with him. Not his dog—he had no pet—but a dog that seemed to materialize out of thin air if you took to running through a field with a stick in your hand. Maybe it was the cornfield's own dog, for its hide was the color of corn husks.

Jim was looking for more trees to conquer. Trees close enough together in size and distance that he might leap from one to the other, but far enough apart to make it a challenge. It was only when he was airborne that he could speak. Not words, maybe, but sound. And that was something. If he could find two perfect trees far enough apart, maybe he could get out a whole sentence. The sentence would be "Where are you, Dad?"

He had stopped speaking when his father went missing. When they found the empty car at the end of a trail deep in the woods. So Jim waited. He waited through the police investigation, through the memorial service, through his mother trying to explain what could not be explained. How in this world could a person just go missing? There didn't seem to be anything left to say.

The cornfield dog took to barking. Caught up in the excitement, that's what Jim thought till he realized that the dog was standing square now, barking at some real enemy. Jim swung around, and there, coming across the rugged ground, was Billy Bones, waving something in his hand. Jim grabbed hold of the end of his long stick, held it up like a pikestaff. Stood, like the dog, square to the invader.

It was not a weapon old Billy was waving. It was paper. Beyond him was the overgrown windbreak that surrounded Billy's shack, and for a moment Jim wondered if he had trespassed on the old man's fields. But the paper wasn't like that, a deed, or whatever, though he waved it like one. He waved it like an accusation at Jim.

"Can you believe it?" he shouted when his wobbly legs had carried him close enough to be heard over the dog's infernal barking. "Can you believe they'd do such a thing?"

Jim wondered if it was the Dee-partment of Highway Robbery again. They had not fixed the road, though Billy had kept up his lonely petition for a week or more. As if his '55 De Soto were a pen, he had written, if not a thousand, at least a few hundred signatures on that road. Jim had even watched him from his bedroom window late one night, traveling up and down, tripping that wire, piling up the numbers.

Now Billy came closer. He was worked up. There was spit hanging out one side of his mouth. Then suddenly he seemed to notice the stick in Jim's hands, and his eyes swam with confusion. He held the paper up to his chest. Jim lowered the stick. The dog stopped barking, sat down. Billy edged closer.

"Can you read, Jim Hawkins? Can you?"

Jim did his statue routine. There was nothing in his eyes but the lowering October sky. Billy dared to step over the last hill of cornstalk rubble that separated them until they were face-to-face. He showed Jim the piece of paper. It was a clipping from a newspaper. There was a drawing at the top, a poor, childish drawing of a poor, mean building. A castle. Above it in handwritten letters it said "Fairyland."

"They're selling it," said Billy, grabbing the clipping back to look at it again. "They're selling Fairyland. There's going to be an auction. Says right here. Can you read, Jim Hawkins?"

Jim didn't say.

"I'll read it to you," said Billy.

FAIRYLAND, ESTABLISHED IN 1912, WILL BE SOLD
BY PUBLIC AUCTION ON NOV. 15, AT 2:00 PM
OPEN HOUSE, NOV. 14

104 acres, has 1.3 km frontage, Trans Canada Highway. Presently 20 acres are developed into an amusement park and consist of a giant playground, 18-hole miniature golf, boating pond, fairy-tale forest, 50-seat miniature train, canteen, souvenir shop, etc., etc.

Billy read the whole thing out loud, looking up furtively from time to time, as if he thought Jim might just decide to hit him with his stick. Jim stood stock-still, listening. His father used to read to him. But nobody had read to him in a long while.

When Billy finished, Jimmy took the advertisement from him and looked it over. It was yellowed.

Fairyland, it turned out, was a long way away. The other end of the country. The owner wished to retire, the clipping said. And the date of the auction was November 15, 1983. The auction had already happened more than a dozen years ago. Jim handed the clipping back to Billy.

Billy looked it over again, shaking his head. His lips were closed tight. One of his teeth poked out the side. He looked away wistfully, checked the clipping one more time. Then he folded it and stuffed it into the chest pocket of his overalls.

The dog suddenly took off. Maybe someone had whistled with a secret dog whistle. Or maybe it had sensed another boy with a stick in some other field.

"Buried a treasure there," said Billy Bones, patting his chest pocket. "In a tin biscuit box, outside the roller-coaster ride."

He looked sideways at Jim, then flinched as if the boy might yell at him for being an idiot.

"I was eleven, about. Your age. We was camping down the road a bit. I snuck out from the tent one night, snuck myself into Fairyland, and buried my treasure. In a biscuit tin. Right outside the roller-coaster ride."

Jim hugged his stick to him, leaned on it. Listened. Far away he heard the cornfield dog barking.

"I drawed a map," said Billy Bones, licking his cracked lips. His eyes were flitting as if in a dream. "I was gonna trick my kid brother. We was gonna *find* that map somewhere. Maybe on the beach near where we was camped. 'Lookit, Johnnie. Lookit here.' And there'd be the map wrapped up in a old piece of cloth, a old piece of oilskin. 'It's a treasure map. Must be a hundred years old, Johnnie.'"

Billy laughed his dry bones laugh. "We'd have ourselves a high old time," he said. "Tracking down that treasure. Tracking it right into Fairyland."

Jim opened his mouth then. No words came out, but Billy seemed to sense he was asking him something.

"What was in it, Jim? Is that what you want to know?"

Billy sniffed. Scratched. He made as if to fish the clipping out of his pocket again, as if maybe there'd be a clue there. "I don't recall, exactly. Not all of it. I know I packed that biscuit tin tight, though." He dug and dug in his memory. Found something. "There was a skull of some small bird. I put a penny in both its eyeholes. I remember that."

He paused, shivered a bit. "I remember that," he said again as if each penny required a separate memory. Then he shook his head. Jim could almost see Billy scrabbling with his old fingers at the top of that buried treasure box. Scratching away the tamped-down earth. Wanting to see

156

inside it again, so far away. Then Billy's arms fell to his sides in defeat.

"I buried the map on the beach," he said. "I had it all set up. We'd find the map and then go after the treasure. And you know what, Jim? My dad packed us up the very next morning, and we left. No one told me why. We left, and we never come back."

He stared at Jim. Cricked his neck a bit as if trying to peer inside Jim's turbulent brown eyes, clear into his head to see what was cooking there. Then he straightened up. Looked around, wrapped his arms about himself as if he'd just realized that it was late in October and too cold to be standing in the middle of a field talking with a silent boy.

"We had come there every summer, Jim. Every danged summer. Now it's gone."

Billy bit on his lip. Then he kicked the ground with his scraped old boot. He hardly made an impression on the dried mud. The frost was already in the ground.

"Fathers do mysterious things," he said.

Then, as abruptly as he had arrived, he turned and marched back toward his place.

◆ ◆ ◆

It snowed late in November, winter knocking on the door. But the seasons weren't about to stop Jim from his quest. He had found himself two perfect trees right on the property line. He looked up, shielding his eyes from the fat, lazy snowflakes. The tops of the trees were two grown men apart. A leap of two grown men. You could fit a whole long sentence into such a jump.

Jim started to climb. He climbed swiftly.

"Look at me, Dad," he said inside his head. "Look at how far I can go." As he clambered from branch to branch, he recalled a summer day when he was little, climbing the apple tree in the yard. His father had stopped fixing the tractor to come and watch. "You scamp," his father said, wiping his greasy hands on a rag. "We should have called you Sir Edmund Hillary."

"Look how high," said young Jimmy. "Look, Dad." He turned to make sure his father was watching. And in that moment of distraction his foot slipped and his hand missed its hold and he fell. But his father caught him.

Jim stopped in his climb, hugged the pine tree tight. With his eyes clapped shut he could smell the grease on his father's hands holding him tight and safe.

The memory passed. He looked down. Directly below, far below, a split rail fence and all along its length thornbushes and piles of stones that his father and his father before that and who knows how many fathers had deposited there, for stones were the biggest crop in this part of the world.

Fence, thornbush, and stone. And nobody to catch him.

He reached the top. He swung the tree angrily, silently swearing at it like a rider on a stubborn animal.

"Take me away from here!" he wanted to say. "Take me away!"

How could there be no clues at all? How could his father just disappear? In mystery books, things were always found: the treasure, the missing person. So if this wasn't a mystery, what was it? Nothing. And what could you say about nothing?

Farther and farther he bent that pine until it fairly whipped him through the snowy air. His eyes squinted through the snowflakes at his treetop target. One, two, three—

He would have leaped for sure if something hadn't caught his eye and made him think a thought outside his anger. Distracted him. Brought him up short.

It was two things, really.

He saw his own house across the field. He saw smoke coming from the chimney. Nothing strange about that. He'd chopped the wood himself. Lighting the morning fire was now his work. But then, as he swayed with greater and greater force, bending the tree to his wild purpose, his eyes took in another chimney, the chimney of Billy Bones's place. He could see it just over the windbreak.

There was no smoke coming out of Billy's chimney.

He stopped. It was like waking up from a nightmare. Suddenly he was frightened and clung to the tree for dear life.

He made his way down and across the cornfield—a treachery of ice—and through the windbreak the way he had seen Billy go. He came out in Billy's yard.

The De Soto was in a shed, covered over with a tarp as if it were Billy's secret destroyer, only called into action to take on the forces of the dee-partments of the world.

The door to the shack where Billy lived was open a bit. Snow filmed the threshold. Jim stepped inside. He had noticed an outhouse, but one whiff inside Billy's shack led him to believe it had been a long time since the old man had made his way out to it. Breathing through his mouth, Jim looked around. The ceiling was low, the windows gummy with grime. In the dimness and the clutter of dilapidated furniture, Jim saw lawn ornaments everywhere. There was a painted gnome standing in the sink, a black boy fishing amid the dirty dishes on the kitchen table. His line hung down to a floor so littered with crumbs that the only thing the black boy was likely to catch was a mouse.

A doe and a fawn leaned against a wall below a coatrack. Billy's greasy plaid jacket had fallen from a hook and hung over the fawn's head, blindfolding it.

Beyond the blinded fawn a door stood slightly open. Jim heard a dry cough. He looked inside. Billy Bones lay in his bed, a comforter up around his ears. His chin was on his chest; his eyes flickered open. He saw Jim, peered at him.

"The wife left," he said. Though his voice was ghostlike, he spoke with such urgency that Jim turned as if he might still catch sight of her leaving. One look at the decrepitude of the front room, however, was enough to tell him that Billy's wife must have left a long time ago. He'd never heard of any wife.

"Took everything," Billy said. "Everything."

Jim stepped into the bedroom. He looked around. He reached out to touch the peeling wallpaper. The wall was glazed with frost.

Billy's chin had fallen to his chest again. Jim turned on his heels and went out of the shack. Beside the porch he found some wood and an ax. He split some wood to kindling, gathered an armful, and set about making a fire in the woodstove. There were piles of aging newspapers handy for tinder. Maybe it was in lighting a fire that Billy had happened upon the news of the sale of Fairyland. Jim didn't stop to read the pages now. Soon he had a good fire going. He checked the chimney for leaking smoke.

He ventured back into the bedroom, over to Billy's bedside. Billy woke up again, though his eyes did not fully open. He licked his lips. Jim went to the kitchen to get him a glass of water. He had to pump the water up. It splashed on the gnome in the sink, brightening to blue a patch of his filthy jersey. Jim poured a cup of the water on the gnome's leg. The dust was washed away to reveal pants as red as the deepest fire. Jim wanted suddenly to wash that gnome and polish it clean. But a cough from the bedroom reminded him why he was there, what he was doing.

Billy had propped himself up in his bed. He reached for the water greedily but sipped at it timidly as if his thirst were a great deal larger than his capacity to swallow. He cleared his throat, spit on the floor. It was still chilly. Jim wondered if the heat from the stove would ever reach this far.

"Left. Just like that," said Billy. He sniffed. "Can you believe it?" His head fell back on the pillow as heavily as if it were filled with plaster. Jim put the glass down on the bedside table. Billy looked longingly at a bookshelf across the room. He slid his arm out from under the covers and pointed with a gnarled finger toward something. Jim followed his gaze and walked over to the bookshelf. He held up one thing after another: an alarm clock, a ship in a bottle, a jar of small change, a book lying open. None of these things was what Billy wanted.

"The box," he said.

On his haunches, Jim explored the shelves. A biscuit tin. He remembered Billy's buried treasure and opened it. There was no bird's skull with pennies in its eyes. There were only stamps.

"Bring it here, Jim."

Jim carried the tin over to Billy, who propped himself up again so he could finger through the contents.

"I used to collect stamps," he muttered. "Collect them proper, in books. There was a stamp club in town, met once a month in the museum there."

He held up a stamp to the pale light coming from his window. It was the face of a man—a president or prime minister. He put it back in the box.

"She took the whole danged thing," said Billy. "The

whole collection. Books and books."

He took a few shallow breaths. Held up another stamp. It was of a black king in tribal robes.

"Sold 'em, I guess. Worth something. You can believe that."

He held up a third stamp, larger than the rest. A triangular stamp, brightly colored.

"Ahhh," said Billy, smiling, "but she didn't get it all."

It was a pirate with flaming red hair. Jim reached out to have a look at it. The pirate had a cutlass raised, a rich gold damask waistcoat and breeches, a gold chain around his neck.

"It's all I got left," said Billy.

Jim looked in the tin, fingered through the stamps. There were other triangular stamps. They were all pirates, six of them. The stamps were from Bermuda.

"They're beauties, eh?" said Billy. Jim nodded. There was Captain William Kidd, Henry Morgan, Edward Teach, known as Blackbeard, Mary Read, Bartholomew Roberts, and Jean Lafitte. Each stamp was a different denomination. Blackbeard's was two dollars.

Billy took the Blackbeard stamp from Jim. He looked at it proudly. "Two Bermuda dollars, Jim. Little red-colored bills, half the size of ours—saw one once." He sniffed. "You could send a parcel anywhere with a stamp like that on it."

Billy handed Jim the stamp. Edward Teach had three pistols in his belt and a glint in his lunatic eyes. His beard was plaited in four braids, laced with gold ribbon.

"When they brung that series out, they called 'em the Bermuda triangles."

Billy Bones took to coughing then. He coughed so much that Jim put the box of stamps down on the bedspread in case he was needed, though he could think of nothing to do to help. When the bout was over, Billy lay back on his pillow exhausted.

Billy looked at him. Looked hard. "What happened to your voice, boy? You lose it somewhere?"

Jim picked up the box of stamps, looked at the Bermuda triangles one by one. Put the top back on the tin. Put the tin back on the shelf where he had found it.

He shuddered, cleared his throat. Opened his mouth, closed it, opened it. He thought of words, gave shape to them with the muscles of his face, his tongue. He took a deep breath. But in the silence just before speech, he heard Billy snore. He shut his mouth.

Jim stoked the fire, piled it high with the driest wood he could find, then turned the damper way down, the better to keep it burning. He opened the icebox to see if there was any food he could leave for Billy beside his bed, but the stench was horrible. He would come back with something from home. Load the fire up again.

He did that for two days, checking on the old man each time. Feeding him a bit of soup. A thermos cup of tea. He discovered other biscuit tins with other treasures in them: buttons, marbles, the wings of butterflies.

The third day he came up the buckled road, he saw an

ambulance at Billy's house. He watched it pull away in a swirl of snow. He stopped in his tracks, wrapping his arms around the pot of soup he'd brought. When the ambulance was out of sight, he went on to Billy Bones's shack. The man was gone. The tin of stamps was gone as well.

He sat at the kitchen table beside the black boy fishing and drank some of the soup. Many-bean soup. One of Mom's specialties. It was good.

◆　◆　◆

Billy Bones died.

"I feel like it's my fault," Jim wrote on the kitchen pad.

His mother shook her head. "You did all you could. As soon as you told me about his condition, I called the district health nurse. They were checking in on him, too, honey."

Jim had been going to talk to Billy. He had felt the words almost come out. Safer to try it on someone not expecting too much, someone touched in the head. Someone who seemed always to be losing things himself.

◆　◆　◆

It was a week after Billy died that a strange thing happened. A parcel arrived for Jim Hawkins, wrapped in brown paper and string. The stamp on it was the two-dollar Bermuda Blackbeard. It had even been canceled at the post office, as if the parcel had really come from Bermuda. There was no return address.

When Mrs. Hawkins handed Jim the package, there was something more than curiosity; there was concern in her eyes. She looked at him as if there were a world of things she didn't know about him, her own son.

Inside the package was the tin box of stamps, including the five remaining pirates. Jim carefully removed Blackbeard from the wrapping paper. He lined the pirates up on his mother's shining table top.

"What is all this then, Jim?" said his mother, stopping to look over his shoulder. Jim gathered his strength together. He opened his mouth, closed it, opened it again. Once again he thought of words, gave shape to them with the muscles of his face, his tongue. He took a deep breath. He leaned out toward the words, reaching, grabbing, squeezing them out of himself into the muffin-smelling air of his mother's kitchen.

"I guess it's a gift," he said.

ACKNOWLEDGMENTS

All possible care has been taken to trace ownership and secure permission for each selection in this series. The Great Books Foundation wishes to thank the following authors, publishers, and representatives for permission to reprint copyrighted material:

Charles, from THE LOTTERY, by Shirley Jackson. Copyright © 1948, 1949 by Shirley Jackson; renewed 1976, 1977 by Laurence Hyman, Barry Hyman, Mrs. Sarah Webster, and Mrs. Joanne Schnurer. Reprinted by permission of Farrar, Straus and Giroux, LLC.

A Bad Road for Cats, from EVERY LIVING THING, by Cynthia Rylant. Copyright © 1985 by Cynthia Rylant. Reprinted by permission of Atheneum Books for Young Readers, an imprint of Simon & Schuster's Children's Publishing Division. All rights reserved.

Podhu and Aruwa, from TALES TOLD NEAR A CROCODILE, by Humphrey Harman. Copyright © 1962 by Humphrey Harman. Published by Hutchinson. Reprinted by permission of the Random House Group, Ltd.

Lenny's Red-Letter Day, from I'M TRYING TO TELL YOU, by Bernard Ashley. Copyright © 1981 by Bernard Ashley. Reprinted by permission of Happy Cat Books Ltd.

Barbie, from BASEBALL IN APRIL AND OTHER STORIES, by Gary Soto. Copyright © 1990 by Gary Soto. Reprinted by permission of Harcourt, Inc.

Ghost Cat, from EERIE ANIMALS: SEVEN STORIES, by Donna Hill. Copyright © 1983 by Donna Hill. Reprinted by permission of the author.

Lucky Boy, from WHAT THE NEIGHBOURS DID AND OTHER STORIES, by Philippa Pearce. Copyright © 1959, 1967, 1969, 1972 by Philippa Pearce. Reprinted by permission of Laura Cecil Literary Agency and the author.

MAURICE'S ROOM, by Paula Fox. Copyright © 1966 by Paula Fox. Reprinted by permission of Simon & Schuster Books for Young Readers, an imprint of Simon & Schuster Children's Publishers.

The Bermuda Triangle, from LORD OF THE FRIES AND OTHER STORIES, by Tim Wynne-Jones. Copyright © 1999 by Tim Wynne-Jones. Reprinted by permission of DK Publishing, Inc. All rights reserved.

ILLUSTRATION CREDITS

Cover art by Terea Shaffer. Copyright © 2006 by Terea Shaffer.

Text and cover design by William Seabright & Associates.

Interior design by Think Design Group.